JEAN-FRANÇOIS BAZIN - MARIE-CLAUDE PASCAL

WONDERFUL DIJON

Translated by Angela Moyon

Photographs

Hervé Champollion

ÉDITIONS OUEST-FRANCE

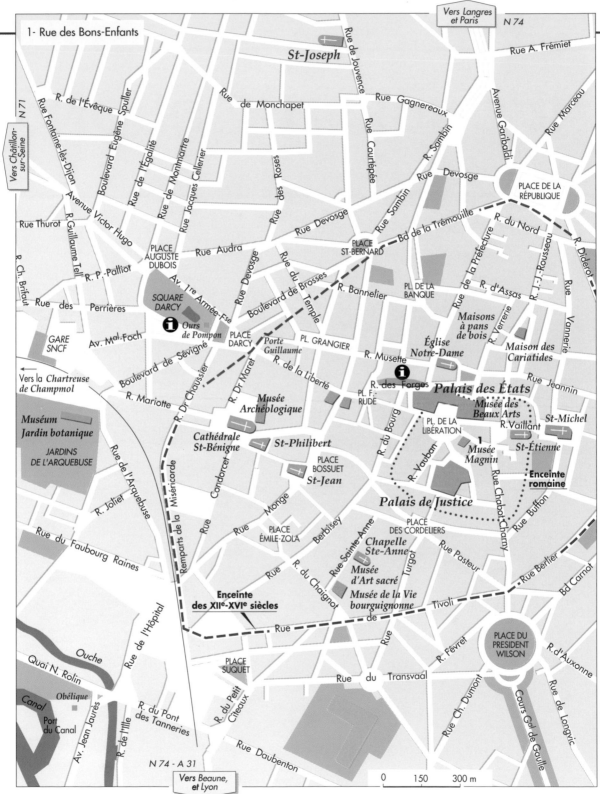

1- Rue des Bons-Enfants

St-Joseph

Vers Langres et Paris — N 74

Rue A. Frémiet

Vers Châtillon-sur-Seine — N 71

Rue de Jouvence

Rue Gagnereaux

Avenue Garibaldi

Rue Marceau

Rue de Monchapet

Rue Courtepée

R. Sambin

Rue Devosge

PLACE DE LA RÉPUBLIQUE

R. de l'Évêque

Boulevard Eugène Spuller

Rue de l'Égalité

Rue de Montmartre

Rue Jacques Cellerier

Rue des Roses

Rue Sambin

Bd de la Trémouille

R. du Nord

R. Diderot

R. J.-J.-Rousseau

Rue Thurot

Avenue Victor Hugo

R. Guillaume Tell

R.-P.-Palliot

Rue Audra

Rue Devosge

Rue du Brosses

PLACE ST-BERNARD

R. de la Préfecture

R. d'Assas

R. Vannerie

PLACE AUGUSTE DUBOIS

R. Bannelier

PL DE LA BANQUE

Maisons à pans de bois

R. Verrerie

Maison des Cariatides

R. Ch. Brifaut

Rue des Perrières

Av. 1re Armée-Fse

SQUARE DARCY

Av. Mal-Foch

Ours de Pompon

PLACE DARCY

Boulevard de Sévigné

Porte Guillaume

PL. GRANGIER

R. Musette

Église Notre-Dame

Rue Jeannin

GARE SNCF

Vers la Chartreuse de Champmol

R. Dr Maret

R. Dr Chaussier

Boulevard de Sévigné

R. Mariotte

R. de la Liberté

R. des Forges

Palais des États

Musée des Beaux Arts

R. Vaillant

St-Michel

Muséum Jardin botanique

JARDINS DE L'ARQUEBUSE

Musée Archéologique

PL. F. RUDE

R. du Bourg

PL. DE LA LIBÉRATION

St-Étienne

Enceinte romaine

Rue de l'Arquebuse

Cathédrale St-Bénigne

St-Philibert

R. Vauban

1 Musée Magnin

R. Chabot-Charny

R. Joliet

Condorcet

Remparts de la Miséricorde

PLACE BOSSUET

St-Jean

Palais de Justice

Rue Buffon

Rue du Faubourg Raines

Monge

PLACE ÉMILE-ZOLA

Berbisey

Rue Sainte-Anne

PLACE DES CORDELIERS

Rue Pasteur

Rue Berlier

Bd Carnot

Rue de l'Hôpital

Rue du Chaignot

Chapelle Ste-Anne

Musée d'Art sacré

Turgot

PLACE DES CORDELIERS

Tivoli

Ouche

Quai N. Rolin

Musée de la Vie bourguignonne

de

Enceinte des XIIe-XVIe siècles

Rue

PLACE DU PRESIDENT WILSON

R. Févret

R. d'Auxonne

Canal

Obélique

Av. Jean Jaurès

R. de l'Ille

R. du Pont des Tanneries

PLACE SUQUET

R. du Petit Cîteaux

Rue du Transvaal

R. Ch. Dumont

Cours Gal de Gaulle

Rue de Longvic

Port du Canal

Rue Daubenton

N 74 - A 31

Vers Beaune, et Lyon

0   150   300 m

Cartographie AFDEC

© 1998 Édilarge S.A. - Éditions Ouest-France, Rennes

SUMMARY

A palette of colours in the tile and slate roofs, broken up by dormer windows and topped with belltowers.

URBAN DEVELOPMENT
WITH A SOUL

All towns like to describe themselves as a major junction.
Yet in the case of Dijon it seems difficult to challenge this description.

A close-up of the ducal palace, Rue des Forges.

The Burgundy upland is brought to a sudden halt by a barrier of limestone. From the top of the Hill (la Côte), the view extends over the Saône Plain to the distant blue-tinged Jura, sometimes even catching a glimpse of the sparkling snow-capped Mont Blanc. Dijon, which forms a break in a monotonous landscape of plateaux on one hand and plains on the other, is where people stop to catch their breath and gather their strength over a convivial meal with a good bottle before setting off again in the direction of one or other of the four cardinal points of the compass. It is a stop-over on the ancient road from Italy to Western and Northern Europe, via the Alps and the Jura. It is a relay on the Agrippan Roman road from Chalon to Langres.

Where does the word **Divio** come from? It probably indicates the presence of a market. Nothing would be more appropriate, given the local character. The village did not grow up on the hilltops of Fontaine or Talant, the normal refuge of an aggressive race; instead it developed in the middle of a dip, in the very place where traffic was at its densest. The people of Dijon in those far-off days sought no quarrel with their neighbours. They were like snails, seeking to pass unnoticed. It comes, then, as no surprise to see that Dijon was not mentioned in any texts until the 6th century, when Gregory of Tours described a large town in the heart of a fertile, cheerful rural environment. Its **castrum**, now marked by plaques indicating its outer walls, once covered the area around the present-day town hall. All that was missing from its thirty-three towers (one of which still exists at 11 and 15 rue Charrue) was a halo of saintliness - and St. Bénigne became the patron saint of the town. A Greek who came from Smyrna with Polycarp, Thyrsus and Andoche c. 150 A.D.? It may be true that Burgundy was evangelised by immi-

A monumental sculpture in the heart of the Petit-Cîteaux district.

grants from Syria or Asia with a Greek cultural background, but this Bénigne, about whom nothing is known, seems to have been invented specifically for this purpose.

During the Dark Ages, the Bishops of Langres settled in Dijon, where they were to stay from the 5th to the 9th centuries.

Refinement in close-up - an old door-knocker.

The Burgundians arrived just at the right time to give a name to this vast region that stretched as far as the eye could see in all directions. But they had made a few detours first. They sailed down from the island of Bornholm in Scandinavia and, in the 1st century A.D., were to be found in Germania. The *Niebelungen* keep alive the legend of this people. But it was thought

preferable to send them off to the borders of the Jura and the Alps, between Switzerland and Savoie. In the 5th century, they created the kingdom of Burgundia, which stretched from Lutèce to Provence, and c. 480 A.D. they captured Dijon. This happy combination of old Gallo-Roman blood and barbarian fervour produced good results, but they were to be short-lived. In the confused centuries of Merovingian rule, Dijon was the setting for a confrontation between Clovis and Gondebaud in the year 500 A.D. The town did its utmost not to get involved in the struggles. It was waiting for its finest hour to strike. "Wait and see" is an old local proverb that can be heard again and again throughout the town's long history. On the occasion of the St. Bartholomew's Day Massacre, for example, the townspeople avoided bloodshed by simply waiting for a counter-order. As for Napoleon's One Hundred Days, the locals merely waited until the tricolour on the spire of St. Bénigne's had faded in the sunshine. Once it had become white, they could give vent to royalist feelings and proclaim, "Long live Louis XVIII"!

Under Charlemagne, Burgundy was scarcely any better off. The Treaty of Verdun (843 A.D.) resulted in the famous subdivision that made the R. Saône a frontier until the reign of Louis XIV. Dijon was only the seat of a modest **pagus**, the forerunner of the balliage system, and the locals made do with this situation for many years. The occupation of Dijon in 1016 marked the start of the Capetian era. So you see, everything comes to he who waits! The town finally became a regional capital under Robert I. The Capetians provided the first ducal lineage in Burgundy, from 1032 to 1361 when Philip of Rouvres died, heirless. The town changed; it started to make progress. The Count had become a Duke. Dijon gained important influence over the other towns in Burgundy such as Autun, Langres, Beaune, or Chalon. Sent to the town by the Abbot of Cluny for this purpose, Guillaume de Volpiano re-established the old St. Bénigne's Abbey, in every sense of the word. The fire of God's word was rekindled in Fontaine, where St. Bernard (1090-1153) was born. He was the saint who was to give Cîteaux its vital thrust forward. He also founded Clairvaux, taking with him the whole of the Christian world, and he set up a new Order. Meanwhile, throughout this period, Dijon kept a watchful eye on its own interests. In or about the year 1185, the town obtained a communal charter. It was able to set up the administration it wanted, and the hospice was founded.

For the first time, the community broke out of its shell, commissioning the building of a new town wall in the 12th century (an area of some 100 hectares, now protected by a preservation order).

Then it fell prey to the storms of History. Who would inherit from Philip of Rouvres? The King of France had a son, who had saved his life at Poitiers, "Father, take care to your left! Father, take care to your right!" The son was called, appropriately, Philip the Bold. He it was who received Burgundy. And whom did he marry? Margaret of Flanders, Philip of Rouvre's fiancee, who brought with her the most intensely-farmed, fertile land in Europe. The Duke of Burgundy became one of the world's great leaders. He and his descendents, John the Fearless, Philip the Good and Charles the Bold, were to upset the course of events throughout Europe for one hundred years. Dijon could not get over it. The town was so retiring, so busily involved in watching its step, so average in everything it did - and events set its head spinning. Capital of the duchy? Why not capital of an entire State? Why not capital of the entire Western world?

The years of thrills and excitement hurtled past like a dream. The Dukes of Burgundy, "Grand Dukes of the Western World", and lords of the best wines in Christianity, actually spent most of their time in Bruges, Ghent, Brussels, Malines, and Courtrai. Dijon was both their cradle (for they were born there) and their final resting-place (they took steps to ensure that they were buried there). It was something

The archway of the William Gate closes off the end of Rue de la Liberté.

The Févret de Saint-Mesmin Residence on Place Bossuet.

The fine frontages in the section of Rue de la Liberté laid out in the 18th century beyond the Palace of States.

The Vogüé Residence in Rue de la Chouette has a luxurious roof of glazed tiles.

The cloisters of the former Bernardine convent house the Museum of Burgundian Life.

of a family home to which they returned occasionally, emotionally sniffing the mustiness in the attic. Charles the Bold left Dijon while very young. Throughout his entire life, he spent less than one week in the town. His daughter, Mary of Burgundy, never set foot in it. Yet people fought in her name in the suburbs of Dijon, for the "Burgundian faith". Dijon accepted this unexpected appointment with good fortune. For such a small town, it was a wonderful breath of fresh air! Wine was exchanged for cloth. The local children had careers. The most ambitious of the locals were given decorations. The old ducal residence became a palace, the Carthusian monastery of Champmol housed the most lavish tombs of the day, and the greatest artists worked there. Although founded in Bruges, the Order of the Golden Fleece had its seat in Dijon's Holy Chapel (1429). It's true that things went badly awry. Charles the Bold clung desperately to an illusion. During his visit to Dijon, he called the town's dignitaries to a meeting which he addressed in a rather surprising manner. He spoke of Lotharingia, "the Middle State", situated midway between a Kingdom and an Empire. He called his entire audience to witness, as he delivered one of the first party political programme speeches in history. He

confirmed his will to revive "the old kingdom of Burgundy, which those in France have long usurped, turning this into a duchy, a fact which its inhabitants must surely regret". Louis XI was too crafty a spider to forget to spin his web around the careless nobleman. But, wounded by the Swiss in Morat and Grandson, the wayward aristocrat was killed beneath the walls of Nancy in 1477. The king elbowed aside his god-daughter, Mary, daughter of Charles the Bold, occupied the duchy and then used the technique of carrot and stick. High society rallied to the new cause. Only the lower classes proclaimed, for the glory of doing so, their attachment to the great dream. For greater security, Louis XI had a castle built in Dijon. It was like a red-hot weal, a searing fleur-de-lys branded on the town's skin. When it was demolished in the latter years of the 19th century, the people of Dijon were delighted. It was almost like a replay of the storming of the Bastille.

It is true that Charles the Bold left nothing in Dijon, not even his father's tomb (the marble had already been bought). His library is now in Brussels, the treasure of the Order of the Golden Fleece is in Vienna, and the spoils of the Burgundian wars are in Bern.

What a fine European dimension for Dijon! Mary married Maximilian of Hapsburg; their grandson was Emperor Charles V. The history of Burgundy, which was linked to the birth of nations in Belgium, the Netherlands, and Luxemburg, took another direction altogether - towards Germany and Austria, or Spain.

Dijon was nothing if not a realist; it became a French town, once and for all.

It acquired the seat of the parliament, a legal and political institution, and brought the Bresse and Bugey areas under its control. These ambitions were better-suited to its temperament than the ideals of the "Great Dukes". Indeed, the statues on their tombs were the only ones to weep for their passing in Dijon. Burgundy was a collection of states and was fairly freely administered under the symbolic control of the Condé family, its governors, and the Intendant, representative of the King and forerunner of today's regional prefects. The Age of Enlightenment was a brilliant per-

iod in the history of Dijon. After Rameau and Bossuet came President de Brosse, Buffon or several great civil engineers. There were the trials of Voltaire and the fame of Rousseau in 1750 after his work, Discourse on the Sciences and the Arts. This was the birthplace of St. Joan of Chantal. Burgundy may be a collection of states but it determined, in a collected manner, to maintain its liberties, manage its own affairs, develop and prosper.

A mediaeval atmosphere in Rue Verrerie, between half-timbered houses and corbelled homes.

The Revolution brought unusual, but limited, bustle to a town of moderates which played host to Carnot, Monge and Guyton de Morveau. Dijon provided France with several geniuses, including the "Organiser of Victory" and the founders of the future Ecole polytechnique. Yet it remained dispassionate in the face of the excesses of the day. Damage was limited to the hammering clean of a few mediaeval sculptures and to the removal of Louis XIV from his horse on the previously-named Place Royale, melted down to produce cannons for the nation. People were guillotined, too, but Dijon was delighted when peace returned. With a population of 20,000 in 1800, the town was taken down more than just a peg or two. It had been a capital. It thought in terms of kingdoms and duchies. It was part of Europe and able to look Paris steadily in the eye.

And eventually it found itself in the position of county town. What good fortune, too, in the name of the département. Côte-d'Or has such a splendid ring to it, much better than Seine-et-Saône or Haute-Seine. But the town had to forget the opulence of the past and accustom itself to life on a smaller, county scale.

Yet Dijon did not give up the struggle and stagnate. Its population was to multiply fourfold over a period of just one hundred years. And in the 19th century Dijon bore little resemblance to other provincial capitals bustling with canons, young ladies in search of a husband, solicitors and poets. It is true that the great minds of the day still followed the R. Seine "up" to Paris - as did Gustave Eiffel, for example. Yet Dijon was not bypassed by the changes that the industrial world brought in its wake, and it coped with progress. Its fountains (a piped water supply to every street corner) soon rivalled those in Italy and, thanks to Henry Darcy, the town became a stop-over on the rail route from Paris to Lyons in 1850 despite the fact that everything pointed to a direct route, avoiding Dijon. Many towns and cities showed a marked lack of interest in the railway, but Dijon gave it its uninhibited support, demanded its presence - and got it. The Burgundy Canal had been replaced by a successor at last and Dijon's star shone brightly in the railroad firmament. Thereafter, the town had to fight against the logical solution - the straight line from Paris to Lyons. It happened again when the motorway was built, and the town managed to obtain the building of the Pouilly-Dijon and Beaune-Dijon links. And again with the coming of the high-speed train when it had to make countless efforts to cling to the new railway line. It succeeded in its bid in 1981. As far as the most predominant of all lines of centralisation is concerned, the Lyons-Paris axis, Dijon always requires a detour, and it has had to re-invent its place as a major junction by highlighting its interests in Switzerland, Lorraine, part of Germany, Savoie and Italy (with the Rhine-Rhône high speed train project running between Dijon and Mulhouse in its first phase). In fact, there are motorways and high-speed train services in all directions!

The lookout turrets in the Legouz de Gerland Residence in Rue Jean-Baptiste-Liégeard.

With their pediments, scrolls and carved uprights, the dormer windows of Dijon offer a dazzling display of ornamentation.

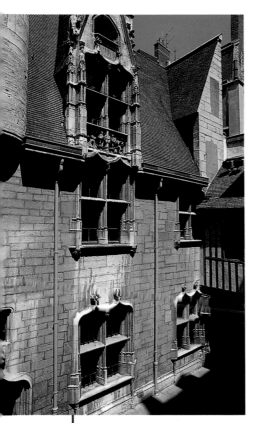

The Chambellan Residence in Rue des Forges, a Flamboyant Gothic masterpiece.

Dijon underwent notable expansion, especially after the Franco-Prussian War of 1870 which changed its outlook (Garibaldi fought within the town, one of the enemy's standards was captured here and, as a result of this important feat of military history, the coat-of-arms acquired the insignia of the Legion of Honour). Numerous people were repatriated from Alsace and Lorraine, bringing an influx of new blood and a taste for business. The border with the enemy was closer than before and Dijon became a fortified town with a string of tiny fortresses and redoubts which, in fact, were never used. It was henceforth a garrison town. Industries developed - Pernot biscuits, Cottereau automobiles, Terrot cycles, Pétolat railroads for use in the mining industry, Lachèze monkey wrenches etc. For the workforce, which arrived from rural districts, it was difficult to find a home in the suburbs. For the second time in its history, Dijon broke out of its shell, demolished its town walls, and, in their place, laid out boulevards in an operation best described as "bastion removal".

Thereafter, Dijon passed through successive armed conflicts unscathed, which explains the richness of its architectural heritage today. Yet the town also went through a period of small-mindedness when nothing was too tiny. The town grew, but there was no town planning, except for the early 1930's when the town council, led by Mayor Gaston Gérard, seemed to have shaken off some of the town's torpor.

Then came Canon Kir. Born in 1876 in Alise-Sainte-Reine, a country priest for most of his life, he became involved in the political struggle in the inter-war period. He gained popularity but at this stage was merely the author of inflammatory articles, and speeches oppositing the government. In 1944, the militia ordered an attack on his life because of his anti-German attitude. Miraculously, he escaped without harm. "Even if I had been killed," he proclaimed, "I should have remained on my feet!" From then on, he was a living embodiment of resistance to the occupying forces. On the Liberation of France, despite the fact that he was then aged 69, he was elected to parliament and became the Mayor of Dijon. The tricolour sash worn by French mayors was to adorn his cassock for twenty-two years. The Canon was a builder, responsible in particular for the development of the university campus, a joint project undertaken with the Rector, Marcel Bouchard, and for the vast hospital complex in Le Bocage. Setting aside his few faults, he had two goods points - he saw life on the grand scale, and he was not averse to dreaming.

Robert Poujade replaced him in 1971. With a very different character, the former student of one of France's foremost higher education institutions (Ecole Normale Supérieure) first undertook a very active policy aimed at equiping the town with open spaces, providing real town planning

The Grand Theatre, built in the early 19th century.

commissioned renovation and projects aimed at showing the town centre off to its fullest advantage. He created new urban districts that retained a human face, forming a stark contrast to the Grésilles and Fontaine d'Ouche estates. He then set about laying out the districts in Pouilly (Toison d'Or Park, a vast complex for shops and leisure amenities, which opened in 1990).

For the past twenty years, Dijon has formed a metropolitan district with its neighbouring communities. There is a population of 150,000 in the town itself and 230,000 including all the outlying districts. The traditional picture of its trades and industries (mustard, blackcurrant liqueur, and spiced loaf) has undergone radical updating. Peugeot produces steering for its cars here. With Fournier, Urgo, Synthélabo and Monot, this is also one of France's major pharmaceuticals centres, as regards both research and production. The Télémécanique company has several plants here.

and supplying sports amenities. He was designated by Georges Pompidou as Minister for the Protection of Nature and the Environment, and was opposed to the general use of concrete and the tentacular growth of towns. He was a forerunner of those interested in the quality of life. He

Main historical events

c. 500 B.C.: The community is one of the staging posts on the ancient route linking the rivers Saône and Seine.

69-70: A camp is built by the 8th Roman Legion

c. 250: Town walls are erected.

c. 400: Dijon replaces Langres as a bishopric (and retains its title until the 9th century)

c. 475: The Burgundians control Dijon.

c. 550: The name «Dijon» appears for the first time (Gregory of Tours).

1031: Robert I, first Capetian Duke of Burgundy.

1137: After a fire, the town walls are rebuilt.

1183-1184: First borough charter (Philip Augustus).

1363: Philip the Bold, first Duke of Burgundy of the Valois dynasty.

1386: The Chamber of Accounts is set up in Dijon.

1477: Louis XI occupies Dijon and the town becomes French.

1513: The Swiss lay siege to Dijon.

1723: The University of Dijon is founded.

1731: Dijon becomes a bishopric.

1789-1790: As a result of the French Revolution, the province of Burgundy no longer exists. Dijon becomes a "county town", the main urban centre in Côte-d'Or.

1808: The Burgundy Canal is opened (St-Jean-de-Losne to Dijon).

1851: The Paris-Dijon railway line is inaugurated.

1870-1871: Dijon is at the heart of the Franco-Prussian War. Garibaldi takes part in the defence of the town.

1887-1897: The castle is demolished. The bastions encircling the old town are removed.

1940-1944: Dijon is occupied throughout the war.

1957: The Montmuzard university campus is opened.

1964: The Lac du Chanoine Kir is created.

1975: The Greater Dijon District is set up.

A carved altarpiece
from the Carthusian
monastery in Champmol.
It can be seen
in the Museum of Fine Arts.

13

BURGUNDY AND ITS PALACE

There is not another town with Dijon's taste for order.
Everything is set fervently in its place and everything
is conscientiously done in its own time.
Yet it would be quite wrong to imagine that fantasy
has no part to play in the life of the town -
and the best example of this fantasy
is the front of the town hall.

Imagine it without the mediaeval tower. You are then faced with a noble building that is a touch too well-behaved, slightly too clean, rather uninteresting because of its symmetry, one might almost say pretentious. It looks like a pork pie - and it lacks verticality. The long exclamation mark formed by the tower breaks up the rather stuffy majesty of the building. It is a source of amazement. It brings a sense of proportion to the building as a whole, both historically and architecturally. For the "Great Dukes" gaze over the entire continent of Europe from the top of their watchtower. They are not on the same level as the members of the parliament or the States, who have their feet firmly on the ground. Yet each age blends with the other; each is respectful of the other. That's Dijon in a nutshell.

"Two palaces that form an intrinsic whole", wrote the historian, Yves Beauvalot. When building began on the present palace in the latter years of the 17th century, nothing was left of the palace commissioned by the Capetian Dukes set hard against the wall of the **castrum**. On the other hand, the palace built for their successors, the Dukes of Valois, had remained almost intact. Philip the Bold, the first of the four "Great Dukes", commissioned the architect Belin de Comblanchien to build the New Tower in 1365. Standing near the Sainte-Chapelle, it is now part of the Art Gallery. It is visible from the **Bar Courtyard** and bears the name **Bar Tower** in memory of René of Anjou, Duke of Bar, who was held prisoner there from 1431 to 1437. "King René" was pretender to the Duchy of Lorraine, future king of Naples and Sicily, and also one of the best-known artists of his day. The staircase adjacent to the tower leads to the gallery built by the Duke of Bellegarde, Governor of Burgundy (1615).

John the Fearless, who was fired by a love of warfare and a desire to conquer

This carved cornucopia
in the Flora Courtyard symbolises
the opulence of an entire era.

On previous page:
The Bar Tower, the oldest part
of the ducal palace,
and the Bellegarde Staircase added
in the 17th century.

Opposite (top):
The Philip the Good Tower.

The Palace of States was built
in the 17th century to designs
by Jules Hardouin-Mansart. Towering
over it is the Philip the Good Tower.

A tour of the palace

Guided tours are available from the Tourist Office in Rue des Forges or on Place Darcy.

Ducal kitchens, Bar Tower: Fine Arts Museum.

Bar Courtyard, main courtyard, Flora Courtyard: open to visitors (unaccompanied visits).

Flora Chamber, Chamber of the States: open to the public during exhibitions or special events (access from the Flora Courtyard). The Gabriel staircase leads to the Chamber of the States.

Chapel of Elected Statesmen: access from the Flora Courtyard.

Philip the Good Tower: access from the passageway between the main courtyard and Place des Ducs.

Mediaeval section of the main building: chamber used for weddings.

Reading room in the municipal archives: access from Rue de la Liberté (unaccompanied visit).

Paris, paid little heed to Dijon. But his son, Philip the Good, took up the work that Philip the Bold had started. He it was who rebuilt the former Capetian palace. In 1433, he turned the kitchens into a veritable temple - the **ducal kitchens**. A whole ox could be roasted in any of the six hearths. Roofed with an eight-ribbed vault supported by a keystone that forms the ventilation shaft, the kitchens are as beautiful as they are functional. Designed to cater for the preparation of the luxurious banquets given by the Dukes, they extended into a bread store and a pastry store, both of which were destroyed in 1853. This is where the town council holds receptions for its numerous visitors, providing them with the aperitif made with white wine and blackcurrant liqueur that Canon Kir made universally famous by giving it his own name.

The main part of the building dates from the 1450's. Designed by an architect from Lyons named Jean Poncelet, a section of it still exists. The covered passageway between the main courtyard and the Dukes' Garden, which locals stroll through every day, the **Hall of Marriages** and the adjacent lobby, the facade overlooking the Place des Ducs (which was laid out to resemble the original in every detail at the end of century) all date from this period. The **Guardroom** is now part of the Art Gallery. Since 1827, it has housed the tombs of Philip the Bold and John the Fearless, brought here from the Carthusian monastery in Champmol.

As to the **Terrace Tower** (or the **Philip the Good Tower**, which the local people insist on calling the "Bar Tower"), it was used as a watchtower and as living quarters. The emblems of Philip the Good, the flint and lighter, decorate the building, which was completed in 1443. It is 149 ft. high, or 169 ft. if you include the lookout post on the top. How many steps are there? Ah, now, there's a question. Count them yourself as you climb.

Charles the Bold was totally uninterested in the residence and it became the King's Palace when Louis XI captured Burgundy. Yet the province retained certain liberties and privileges, in particular the right to determine and collect direct taxes payable to the monarch. This was an area of States. After 1688, the States of Burgundy (clergy, nobility and third estate) met in Dijon every three years and were chaired by the Governor. Between sessions, a permanent executive council governed the affairs of the province. The States General represented the three orders. They required office buildings, which they were granted permission to build within the walls of the King's Palace.

Building started on the **Palace of the States** in 1681; it was to last for one hundred long years. An architect from Paris, Daniel Gittard (1625-1686) and his assistant, Martin de Noinville, soon oversaw

the construction of the **States Building** (with the Chamber of States on the upper floor and miscellaneous rooms on the ground floor). In 1685, the members elected to the States General decided to adorn the esplanade in front of the palace with an equestrian statue of Louis XIV. They dreamt of having their own Place Royale. The Prince of Condé, who was duly consulted, recommended Jules Hardouin-Mansart, one of the main architects behind Versailles, and designer of two new squares in Paris (Place Vendôme and Place des Victoires).

Jules Hardouin-Mansart (1646-1708) took over the design work for the entire development. He designed the

entrance hall to the States Building, which is decorated with pilasters and statues of *Strength* and *Vigilance* carved by Etienne Masson. For the facade, he used the model of the gateway designed by Daniel Gittard leading to the main courtyard in the King's Palace. Etienne Masson carved *Glory* and *History writing down the King's achievements*. The Palace of States was completed in 1689. At the same time, the **Place Royale** passed beyond the design stage and was built on the esplanade. Semi-circular arcades, a balustrade, what a marvellous backcloth for a sculpture! In 1686, the elected members of the States General commissioned Etienne Le Hongre (1628-1690), one of the best sculptors to have worked on Versailles, to carve the *equestrian statue of Louis XIV*. Completed in 1690, the sculpture was brought by river to Auxerre in 1693, but transport proved difficult and costly and the statue remained in a shed in a small village near Auxerre for more than twenty years. It finally reached Dijon in 1720, was inaugurated in 1725, and was sma-

The ribbed vaulting in this mediaeval chamber in the Palace of States is beautiful for its purity of line. The chamber has become a public passageway linking the Square des Ducs and the main courtyard.

Below: The tomb of Philip the Bold.

Paid twice by the Burgundians

The Palace of the States of Burgundy had just been completed when the French Revolution broke out. The provinces and corresponding administrative structures were abandoned and the vast buildings no longer served any purpose. They were confiscated by the State by virtue of the law on national property. In 1831, Dijon had to buy them back in order to use them as the Town Hall. This means that the people of Burgundy had to pay for the palace twice.

The majestic staircase designed by Gabriel leads up to the Chamber of States.

decided in favour of the Tower. The new buildings were erected between 1689 and 1700. The Terrace Tower had been saved but all the other older sections were demolished, concealed or integrated into the new palace. The architect was also responsbile for the interior decoration of the central part of the building - magnificent wood panelling, chimneybreasts decorated with **bas-reliefs in honour of Louis XIV** designed in Versailles and carved in Dijon by Jean and Guillaume Dubois (victories over the Austrians and Spaniards, the Peace Treaty of Nijmegen, Jason conquering the Golden Fleece and the King's hope of recovering the Order that had passed into the hands of the Hapsburgs, and Louis XIV stamping out heresy after the Revocation of the Edict of Nantes). These works of art are in the chambers on the first floor (Condé salon, the mayor's office and his spokesman's office).

Robert de Cotte (1656-1735) who took over from Jules Hardouin-Mansart as Royal Architect, continued the work for the Prince of Condé, Governor of Burgundy. An example of his work is the woodpanelling in the reception room, later the landing on the staircase leading to the Mayor's Office (1710).

shed by revolutionaries in 1792 in order to be melted down to make cannons in Le Creusot.

The old King's Palace, which overlooked the new Place Royale, was something of an architectural hotchpotch. Jules Hardouin-Mansart designed the palace we see today but the Terrace Tower stood in the way of his plans. There was no place for this Gothic construction amidst his orderly piece of Classicisim. Yet the whole population of Dijon was fired with a will to save the threatened building. The King was asked for his opinion and he

---

The four Great Dukes of the Western World

Philip the Bold (1342-1404): Youngest son of the King of France, John the Good. He was granted Touraine (Loire Valley) but preferred Burgundy (1364) after the death of the last Duke of the Capetian line, Philippe de Rouvres. Philip the Bold was a Valois. He married Margaret of Flanders and founded the dynasty that bore his name, opening Burgundy to Flanders and creating a great destiny. His motto was *Il me tarde* or *Moult me tarde* (I am impatient). He was buried in Dijon.

John the Fearless (1371-1419): Although born in Dijon, he was more a man of Flanders than a Burgundian and he showed scant interest in his birthplace. He launched into the war that opposed the Armagnac and Burgundian factions, tried an alliance with England, and aimed at seizing power in France and gaining control of Paris. He died at the bridge in Montereau. His motto was *Ic houd, Je ne cède pas, je tiens!* (I yield not, I hold good!). He was buried in Dijon.

Philip the Good (1396-1467): Born in Dijon but steeped in Flemish culture, he showed a passionate interest in the State of Burgundy and became the most influential patron of the arts in the Western world. He founded the Order of the Golden Fleece and became enamoured of Dijon. He was a Grand Duke of the Western World in every sense of the term. His motto was *Auttre n'auray* (I shall have none other). His emblems were a flint and the lighter used to prime firearms. He was buried in Dijon but his tomb was never built.

Charles the Bold (1433-1477): Born in Dijon, the son of Isabella of Portugal, Philip the Good's third wife. He dreamt of rebuilding Lothringia as it had been in the days of Charlemagne's sons. He wanted to create a State midway between empire (Germany) and kingdom (France) and be crowned king. He was a poor warlord and an inefficient politician compared to Louis XI. Because of his inefficiency, the Duchy of Burgundy was lost at the battles of Grandson, Morat and Nancy where he died on the battlefield. He was buried in Bruges.

Mary of Burgundy (1457-1482): Mary was the only daughter of Charles the Bold and the wife of Maximilian of Austria. She united the Valois of Burgundy and the Hapsburgs. Her grandson was Emperor Charles V. She tried to rally her subjects in 1477 by a letter steeped in pathos, «I pray that their courage may always include faith in Burgundy even when obliged to speak otherwise». Franche-Comté was part of her inheritance and became Spanish. It remained so until the reign of Louis XIV. Mary died at a young age after a fall from a horse and was buried in Bruges. She never visited Dijon.

The **Chamber of States** was first used for the provincial assembly in 1700. A gallery enabled visitors to follow the proceedings. There was a dais for the governor and tiers of seats. Wall hangings decorated with Burgundy's coat-of-arms were placed round the walls in 1768. After the French Revolution, the hall was used as a school room, a concert hall, a ballroom and a reception room. Prince Louis Napoleon gave his most famous speech there, announcing the coup d'état of 2nd December 1848 to "those with ears to hear". Restored in 1895 in line with the style of the day, the Chamber of States was given the re-mounted canvases that cover its ceiling and serve as a mild token of the Arts. The main painting, *"The Glories of Burgundy"* by Henri-Léopold Lévy (1896) is remarkable for its limewood frame covered in gold leaf which was made by a sculptor named Hiolle. The work of art, which has recently been restored, reminds the people of Dijon that they have every reason to be proud of their province. Since the day members of the French Resistance were sentenced to death here in 1944, the chamber has never been used as a ballroom.

Jacques Gabriel (1667-1742) continued the work. Built between 1733 and 1738, the **"Gabriel Staircase"** leads to the Chamber of States. "The finest staircase in France", say the people of Dijon. And it is indeed difficult to imagine anything with more elegance and majesty. The

The Palace of States is Classical and grandiose, in the manner of Versailles.

scraps of trophies on the walls indicate the beneficial actions of the States while the arms of France are carried by two angels illustrating *Glory* and *Fame*.

Thereafter Jacques Gabriel moved on to build the superb **Chapel of Elected Members** in 1738 and 1739. The decoration on the doors and stone panels amazes visitors by the profusion of Rococo ornamentation associated with the rigour of the Classical mind. A local sculptor, Claude Saint-Père, who carved the woodpanelling in the **Meeting Room of the States** (now the municipal archives) to designs by Pierre Le Mousseux in 1736, was chosen by Jacques Gabriel, along with the architect from Versailles, Jacques Verberckt, to carve the reredos in the chancel.

The **buildings in the Flora Courtyard**, which gets its name from the horns of plenty on the North Gateway (1776-1780), are a wonderful example of the Louis XVI style.

The **Flora Chamber** on the first floor was decorated in 1780 to designs by a painter named François Devosge. The walls are painted to resemble marble, and the windows are topped by military trophies recalling the victories of the House of Condé. The trophies are made in stucco work that resembles bronze.

The East Wing was designed by Charles-Joseph Le Jolivet between 1782 and 1786. The palace was no sooner completed than the French Revolution broke out.

The States of Burgundy

In pre-Revolutionary France, Burgundy was a «State» i.e. it enjoyed the privilege of raising taxes and administering its own affairs. The States General of the province drew on the three orders for members (clergy, nobility, third estate). From 1668 onwards, they met every three years at meetings chaired by the Governor (the family of the Princes of Condé).

Between these three-yearly meetings, the province was administered by a permanent committee (General Elected members) made up of a representative of the clergy, a representative of the nobility, two representatives of the third estate but with only one vote (one of them was obligatorily the Mayor of Dijon), a representative of the monarch and two members of the Chamber of Accounts. Since the work of the General Elected members expanded and required increasing numbers of staff, new premises were needed. It was therefore decided to build the Palace of States.

Work began in 1681 in the King's Lodging, the former palace of the Capetian Dukes (nothing is now known about this palace) and the old palace of the Valois Dukes (of which extensive remains have survived).

"AH! THE FINE TOWN WITH THE ONE HUNDRED BELLTOWERS..."

*Who made that statement as he gazed at Dijon? Henri IV or François I?
Probably neither of them, but it's of no importance.*

Many of the towers disappeared in the 18th century; others were swept away on the tide of the Revolution or because of the prevailing lack of interest in the country's heritage during the last century. So many towers, gone for ever! One of Napoleon's Ministers, Emmanuel Crétet, who called himself Count of Champmol, purchased the Carthusian monastery that had been

On previous pages:
Notre-Dame Church
in the heart of the old town.

Right: A close-up of the Moses Well.

The moving sculptures on the entrance to Champmol Church were produced by Claus Sluter.

set up by Philip the Bold at the entrance to Dijon in order to provide himself and his Valois descendents with a burial ground. It was the St. George's Chapel of the Dukes of Burgundy, one might say. Champmol was a melting pot of European arts in the late 14th century, attracting Claus Sluter, Claus de Werve, Antoine Le Moiturier, Jean de Marville, and Juan de La Huerta. And it was this masterpiece that served as a source of building stone. The monastery was demolished and its treasures dispersed far and wide. Of **Champmol Church** built in 1383 then demolished and rebuilt c. 1840, all that remains is the doorway designed by Jean de Marville and decorated by Claus Sluter. Flanked by St. John and St. Catherine, Duke Philip and his Duchess, Margaret of Flanders, already provide a foretaste of the figures on the monument built just a few yards away by a carver from Holland - the famous **Moses Well**, which once stood in the small cloisters in the Carthusian monastery. Only Moses steadily returns the gaze of Michaelangelo's prophet. He is God's ram; rays flow from his forehead while light gives his skin a distended appearance. He really is the enlightened prophet, proclaiming the future. Claus Sluter probably remembered the Jewish beggars he had seen in Holland when he carved the face and

21

Have you touched the owl?

This is the question on everybody's lips in Dijon the night before an exam, or the morning of a wedding. In short, at the time of all the most important events in any-body's life.

The small stone owl is the good luck charm of an enti-re town. It sits on one of the flying buttresses of Notre-Dame Church, in the aptly-named Rue de la Chouette (in French, «chouette» means «owl»). It is open to question whether it was the architect's trade mark or that of a master stonecarver. Take a look and linger awhile. You are almost sure to see a house-wife on her way home from the market, a police officer, a couple in love, or a bunch of tourists stop on the way past and give the bird that symbolises wisdom an affectionate stroke while they make a wish.

St. Philibert's, the only Romanesque church in Dijon.

stance of Isaiah, Jeremiah and the others, all of them under the protection of the angels whose gestures have all the charm of childhood.

In 1802, demolition work began on Dijon's **Sainte-Chapelle**, a gem of Gothic archi-tecture and the seat of the Order of the Golden Fleece. Built in accor-dance with a vow taken by Duke Eudes III of Burgundy, who had sur-vived a terrible storm as he made his way home from the Holy Land in 1172, the Sainte-Cha-pelle was completed in the late 14th century. The ruby red glow of its stained-glass windows was so bright that it was commonly com-pared to the colour of Chambertin wine. The choir stalls bore the coats-of-arms of the Knights of the Golden Fleece. The Spanish colours captured in Rocroi dra-ped its walls. The holy wafer was a gift from the Pope. The children's choir brought sparkle to services. And it all disappeared, sold off by auction, pillaged, destroyed. The Theatre (1810-1828) now stands on the site once occupied by the cloi-sters of the Sainte-Chapelle.

Luckily there are still a great many belltowers left in Dijon. Ten centuries of religious archi-tecture. Built in the mid 12th century on the site of a Mero-vingian basilica, **St. Philibert's Church** was one of those Romanesque churches whose nave and side aisles are roofed with groined vaulting. The door-way in the south aisle (on the Rue Danton) still has its rich carvings. As to the main door-way, it dates from the 13th cen-tury. The central section of the porch is more recent (15th cen-tury), as are the side arches (dating from the Classical per-

iod) and the chapels along the left-hand side (second half of the 18th century). The Flamboyant Gothic stone **belltower** dates from the early 16th century. The parish of St. Philibert's was once said to be the busiest one in the town, and the one with the greatest sense of civic duty. It was here that the Mayor of Dijon was proclaimed and around it lived the "blue bottoms", the turbulent corporation of winegrowers.

The church was deconsecrated during the French Revolution and used for anything and everything - as a salt-peter warehouse, stables etc. It was badly damaged in 1825 and the apse and two apsidal chapels were demolished to leave way for the unnecessary, and tiny, Rue des Vieilles-Etuves. Left to decay for many years, there was a glimmer of hope for St. Philibert's when the town council began to restore it in the early 70's. The church was soon reopened as an exhibi-tion and concert hall. Unfortunately the underfloor heating dried out the pillars which had been impregnated with salt-peter and the urine passed by the horses once stabled there. The stone began to

flake away and the church had to be closed again.

St. Bénigne's is the minster of a monastery founded in the 6th century when the cult of St. Bénigne began to spread. The original Merovingian basilica was replaced in 870 A.D. by a new basilica. When it, in turn, began to decay, it was rebuilt soon after the year 1,000 A.D. by St. William. He is known to the people of Dijon as William of Volpiano but the Italians call him William of Dijon! Born near Novare in 962 A.D., he was a monk in Cluny then Abbot of St. Bénigne's where he re-established order and discipline and laid the basis for the spread of the monastery's influence. The first stone of the new building was laid in 1001 A.D.; it was followed by many, many more stones over the next twenty years. At that time, it was one of the finest Romanesque buildings in existence. Beyond the chancel was a circular three-storey church (the St. Bénigne Rotunda), built over the tomb crypt. The upper storeys were unfortunately demolished in 1792 and the crypt was filled in. Rediscovered in 1843 and restored, the mysterious secret crypt is now all that remains of the vast Romanesque minster. In 1271, a tower collapsed, demolishing the chancel. Abbot Hugues d'Arc then undertook to rebuild the church completely. The present building, on which work began in 1280, was completed early in the 14th century and it has survived to this day, almost unscathed. The most extensive alterations date from 1896 when a wonderfully slender spire was built above the transept crossing. An architect named Charles Suisse flung it skywards. Its tip is 302 ft. above ground level and there is an unsupported pyramid 179 ft. high above the roof. The people of Dijon are more than a little proud of having the bravest cockerel in France, perched on the top. The slope of the hip-rafter is pushed to a maximum in this construction. Any additional angle of slope and the rafters would not be able to remain level, nor would the roof stand up to the wind. Nowadays, a century later, the prodigious piece of architecture is still in place. One regrettable incident was the hammering clean of the statues and the tympanum above the main doorway in 1794. This disfigured mediaeval tympanum was replaced during the days of the Napoleonic Empire by the tympanum from the old St. Stephen's Cathedral, which explains why the carving of *The Martyrdom of St. Stephen* by Jean-Baptiste and Edme Bouchardon (1720) is actually to be seen on St. Bénigne's. The former minster became a cathedral during the Revolution, replacing St. Stephen's. Among

Left. St. Bénigne's Church dominates the urban landscape.

St. Bénigne's Church illustrates all the refinement and verticality of the Gothic period.

A close-up of stained glass in Notre-Dame.

Right:
Notre-Dame.

Right: Notre-Dame.
St. Bénigne's Church:
the superb 11th-century crypt
and its ninety-six pillars visible
in the dim lighting.

its Bishops were Albert Decourtray, before he was nominated to Lyons as Primate of France and, later, as Cardinal. As to the neighbouring Archaeological Museum, it is housed in the former Benedictine dorter.

The religious soul of Dijon is to be found in **Notre-Dame**, a strange church to be sure, full of tales to tell and secrets to keep. Built between 1210 and 1240, it is the West Front that is the most surprising feature of the church. It consists of three arches above which are two storeys of arcading decorating a vast expanse of wall between two turrets above piers. The unusual character of these colonettes would perhaps have paled into insignificance had mediaeval sculptors not had the idea of covering them with fake **gargoyles** on three rows of string-courses adorned with foliage. The gargoyles form a motley crew, like civilisation itself and, no doubt, the population of more heavenly spheres. There are virtues and vices, gluttony and the condemned soul, scandalmongering and avarice, goodness and charity, an eagle and a monkey. Destroyed over the years (one of them is said to have fallen off the wall and crushed a money-lender of all people), all the gargoyles were recarved in 1881 by a sculptor named Lagoule. Only the carving at the very top on the right hand side is a copy of the original carving (and the original is to be seen in the Art Gallery). Having been an English assistant in the Carnot High School in Dijon, Henry Miller devoted a fabulous page of writing to the gargoyles in his *Tropic of Cancer*.

In the chapel to the right is **Our Lady of Hop**e. Thought for many years to be a black Virgin, the statue's original colours were brought back to life in 1947 by Pierre Quarré. The statue was once covered in heavy clothing and could scarcely be seen. Now it can be seen in its emotionally moving nudity. Carved in the 11th century in the same style as the Golden Majesty of Clermont-Ferrand, this is the oldest wooden statue of the Virgin Mary to have been carved in France. And Dijon

has twice been liberated on the same date after a novena was said to Our Lady of Hope - from the Swiss in 1513 and from the Germans in 1944.

St. Michael's Church in Rue Vaillant is striking for its Renaissance West Front. The architect seems to have wanted to prove his absolute knowledge of the orders of Antiquity, as if it were a masterpiece designed by a journeyman applying for membership of a trade-guild. It dates from the late 16th century. The two lantern turrets (1667) look rather strange above the building - like two nightcaps. Built from 1497 onwards, the

church nevertheless belongs to the Flamboyant Gothic period. But the years passed and the building work progressed very slowly, so that by the time the West Front was to be built, the Renaissance had arrived! From the south portal (on the right) to the north portal, the evolution of architectural styles is obvious. Fortunately, the carvings on the portals were not damaged in 1793 like the ones in Notre-Dame. The Revolutionaries held their services in St. Michael's, which benefitted from their protection. From Gothic to Classicism, from religious themes to the myths of Antiquity - what an extraordinary variety! The Last Judgement on the tympanum above the main doorway was carved by Nicolas de la Cour (1551).

Nearby is the former **St. Stephen's Church**, which was a cathedral for a few decades during the 18th century when

the seat of the bishopric was changed from Langres to Dijon. Since 1896, it has been the headquarters of the Chamber of Commerce and Industry, after a period as a grain store. Built in the mid 11th century and altered in the 15th, it was originally an Augustinian abbey church. The chancel and transept are now in premises close by, near the crypt of the church (1077) and the old town wall (3rd century). Now occupied by the Chamber of Commerce and Industry, the nave dates from the second half of the 17th century. The West Front was designed by Claude Martin de Noinville (1720). As to the original tympanum, it now decorates St. Bénigne's Church.

Tastefully and discreetly accomplished, this re-use of a historic monument is reminiscent of the former **St. John's**

St. Stephen's, now the Chamber of Commerce and Industry.

Left:
Notre-Dame Church, an amazing west front marked out by the slender arcading between three rows of fake gargoyles.

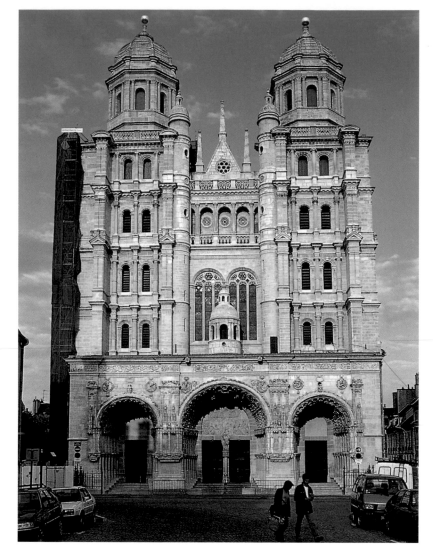

St. Michael's Church: tracery
in stone resulting from
a combination of Gothic and
Renaissance architecture.

Our Lady of Hope.

Church on the Place Bossuet, now a
theatre called Le Parvis Saint-Jean.
Bossuet, who was christened in the
church, is no doubt required to change
his severe opinion of actors... Built on
the site of a basilica dating from the end
of the Roman Empire, this mid 15th-cen-
tury church lost its spires during the
French Revolution. Its chancel was removed a few years later to give more space
for the square. The church was turned
into a covered market in the 19th century, returned to the Church in 1862, again
de-consecrated in 1972 and, since then,
St. John's has enjoyed a new life, without

dwelling on its past history *(it houses
Théâtre national de Dijon-Bourgogne* under
the direction of Dominique Pitoiset).

Other examples of the re-use of old
churches and chapels include the **Godrans
Chapel** designed by Father Martellange
(c. 1610), part of a Jesuit college founded in 1581 by Odinet Godran, which
has been used as the library's reading
room since 1909 (Rue de l'Ecole-de-
Droit); and **St. Anne's Chapel**, built c.
1700 and once part of a Bernardine
convent (circular nave and dome reminiscent of the Salute in Venice), now a
Museum of Sacred Art (Rue Saine-

The former St. John's Church is now a theatre.

Anne). Of the **Carmelite Chapel** in the Rue Victor-Dumay, all that remains is the West Front built early in the 17th century and its decorative features ascribed to Jean Tassin. The convent was closed during the French Revolution and turned into a barracks before becoming the head office of the Greater Dijon Council.

The **Protestant church** on the Boulevard des Brosses was designed by Félix Paumier to resemble a mediaeval church and was built in 1898. The **synagogue** (Rue de la Synagogue) was built in 1879 to designs by Alfred Sirodot, in a Romano-Byzantine style. As for the **mosque** in the Rue Charles-Dumont, it dates from the 1980's.

The **Sacré-Cœur** on the Place Général Giraud in the Maladière District was designed by an architect named Julien Barbier who, with Mgr Tattevin, expressed a wish to create a veritable monument in this new urban district. A vast triple-spanned nave, a wide transept, a semi-circular chancel and an external baptistery were built between 1933 and 1938. **St. Bernadette's Church** (Boulevard des Martyrs de la Résistance) was built in 1964 in the Grésilles District, to designs by Belmont. It consists of a vast nave over a semi-underground crypt. The roof is shaped like a pagoda and the building makes use of steel, aluminium and plastic. There is a campanile with a tall spire 114 ft. high. More recent still, **St. Bernard's** (Boulevard Alexandre Iᵉʳ de Yougoslavie) is a huge elongated nave running into a chancel with a flat chevet. The spirit of the Cistercians is adapted to suit the use of concrete and great expanses of bare stone wall, in accordance with designs by Alix Sorin (1958-1959). Even more recent is the **Church of Elizabeth of the Holy Trinity** in the Fontaine d'Ouche District, built in 1985 to designs by Jacques Prioleau. This church is dedicated to a Carmelite nun from Dijon (1880-1906) who was beatified in 1984.

Jack-o'-the-Clock and his family

Jacquemart is the oldest animated clock in France, with the ones in Paris and Sens. It was originally part of the belfry in Courtrai where it rang out the hours but, in punishment for the Flemish rebellion, Philip the Bold had it taken down, packed up and sent to Dijon where he handed it over as one of the spoils of war in 1382. In fact, it is History's oldest «displaced person»!

Since the people of Dijon had no belfry, they mounted the Flemish clock on Notre-Dame Church. It is there, for more than six hundred years, that the figure has been philosophically smoking his pipe and striking the hours just as he used to do in Courtrai, while he keeps a watchful eye on the locals. In an attempt to brighten up his lonely existence, the people of Dijon gave him a wife, Jacqueline, in the 17th century followed by a son, Jacquelinet, in 1716 and a daughter, Jacquelinette, in 1881. They have not yet understood the (sound) effect that a third child would have on the couple in the 20th century.

The «Three Faces House» in Rue de la Liberté.

THE WORK
OF CENTURIES,
OR THE SONG OF THE STONE

There are several routes into Dijon and each provides a different view of the town.

The south consists of a huddle of buildings and blocks of flats which sprang up without any masterplan; an attempt has been made to bring order into the chaos. The Canal Harbour sets the tone for the renaissance. There is a wink at tradition with the varnished roof tiles set out to form diamond shapes. To the west is the Avenue Victor-Hugo, a stretch of Art Nouveau apartment blocks. The balconies and carvings full of flowing, liana-like movements are brought to an abrupt halt by the Haussmannian austerity of the Cloche and the Place Darcy.

Lower down is the railway station whose spidery web of lines and cables spreads as far as St. Bénigne's. This is a culture shock immortalised by the writer, Henri Vincenot.

If you enter the town from the north, you will travel through Time, from the Golden Fleece district with its science parks, leisure complexes and hypermarkets to the younger Clémenceau District,

set between marker buoys that are, in fact, the academy of music that shines like copper and the repressive mass of the Law Courts. The Place de la République provides two routes to the old town. The aristocratic side is the Rue de la Préfecture; the hail-fellow-well-met side takes in the Rue Jean-Jacques Rousseau which opens onto a fake picture of Dijon glistening in the sunshine, in fact a mural painted by Dominique Maraval. On the eastern side, the town fades out into the Saône Plain, without quite realising what is happening to it. The former Montmuzard Estate has become a residential district. The streets run down to the boulevards and roundabouts in the Place du Trente Octobre and the Place Wilson. The "Fine Ramparts" (Tivoli) that once encompassed the town are now no more than a memory. Dijon, "that deliciously melancholy, gentle town"? Every year, in the spring, Victor Hugo's description is brought back to life

A close-up of the Caryatids House.

The moving beauty of a mediaeval statue worn smooth by the passing years in Rue Amiral-Roussin.

Opposite (right): A half-timbered house in Rue de la Chouette.

Below: The mediawal atmosphere of Rue de la Chouette.

Mediaeval towers, the lighthouses of power

The old town centre in Dijon was reshaped by successive building projects, in particular during the 18th century. Behind this Classical façade is a prestigious mediaeval architectural heritage in which the characteristic features are easily recognisable viz. the predominance of vertical constructions in the form of towers on the ducal palace and turrets on aristocratic mansions. These were strong points designed as symbols of power.

All around the palace, leading administrators who shared the lives of the dukes and rich bourgeoisie commissioned wonderful freestone townhouses which are outstanding for both their layout and their decoration. The buildings overlooking the courtyards set back from the street were linked to the main apartments by traceried wooden galleries. A spiral staircase led to the upper floors, a style which became increasingly common in the 15th century. The stairs were frequently built into the tower that flanked most mediaeval mansions and that was reminiscent of a mediaeval watch-tower. Having lost its original purpose, it became a vital symbol of status and authority.

There are fifteen or more such towers in the old town centre, often topped by a small roof or traceried balustrade. Some were added to buildings; others were an integral part of the house. Some overlook the street; others the courtyard. All of them have a characteristic outline and are symbols of a historical period.

for a brief instant when the trees on the Place Wilson take on a gauze-like appearance and entwine the bandstand of another age in the whorl of their white and pink blossom. The ramparts were demolished in the late 19th century, and replaced by boulevards. A necklet of tarmacadam in place of a necklet of walls. The town gained space in which to breathe without losing its atmosphere. It has gained its present appearance, unaffected by major upsets in history, gliding smoothly down the passing years. Immovable beneath its stone shell...

The days of the Great Dukes

In memory of its mediaeval history, St. Bénigne's, Notre-Dame, and St. Philibert's jut up above the skyline, like prestigious capital letters. But they are counterbalanced by the Terrace Tower, the symbol of the other form of power - temporal might v. religious authority. The Great Dukes brought Dijon its first golden age, giving it in just one century a vitality that could have made it a capital city. The dream may have ended in 1477 but the wheels had been set in motion. The architecture was already of a very high standard. Henri Chambellan, Mayor in 1490, commissioned for himself one of the first mansions worthy of the name, in the Rue des Forges. It is a gem of Flamboyant Gothic architecture with tall dormer windows, a traceried balustrade and a spiral staircase that resembles a piece of lacework in stone. Not far away is the Morel-Sauvegrain Residence, built in the 15th cenutry for a Captain whose mother was Charles the Bold's wet nurse. This is an important historical reference and is typical of a town whose entire history is based on a tangle of marriages and descendents.

Overlooking the Place des Ducs, are the splendid Flamboyant Gothic windows of the

The statue of the "Bareuzai" keeps watch over Place François-Rude.

Dijon through the years

Mediaeval Houses:
10 rue de la Chouette: Millière House
54 rue de la Liberté: House of Three Faces
2 rue Auguste-Comte: House of Three Gables
Rue Verrière: rows of half-timbered houses on each side of the street
31 rue Amiral-Roussin
34 rue des Forges: Chambellan Residence

Renaissance houses and mansions:
38 rue des Forges: Maillard House
1 rue Chaudronnerie: mansion
28 rue Chaudronnerie: Caryatids House
23 rue Amiral-Roussin: Fyot de Mimeure Residence
16 place des Ducs: Berbis Residence

The porch in the old Church of St. Mary Magdalen in Rue Amiral-Roussin (close-up).

**The ducal Court, a centre
of European artistry**

Dijon, located between Paris and
Avignon, between the regions of Berry
and Savoie, and halfway between Italy
and Flanders, enjoyed a vital geographical situation during the Middle Ages. The
Dukes of Burgundy commissioned artists
from all over Europe to work on their
constructions.

The best-known were Claus Sluter,
Claus de Werve, Jean de La Huerta,
Antoine le Moiturier, and Jean de
Beaumetz. Most of them also worked for
other prestigious patrons of the day. The
best-known architect to Philip the Bold,
Drouet de Dammartin, worked on Charles
V's Louvre with Raymond du Temple. He
also received a commission from the Duc
de Berry.

All trades were involved in the projects - architects, stonemasons, slaterers,
tile layers, sculptors, painters, master glass
painters, illuminators, embroiderers, gold-
smiths, and tapestry weavers. Some were
local but others travelled some consi-
derable distance, from Troyes, Bar-sur-
Aube, Compiègne, Angers, Orléans, La
Rochelle and Avignon, or even from Spain
and, more importantly, Flanders.

Rue de la Liberté is the main
shopping street cutting
through the town centre
and is always crowded.

Ducal Palace. It is a sophisticated form of Gothic script, which Victor Hugo compared to the castle in Blois. The buildings all round the palace express their mediaeval heritage in other ways. Subtly, in the winding streets like the Rue des Forges, or in the narrow houses for, tiny as one's home might be, every self-respecting burgher had to have his own house front on the street in the Middle Ages, and building land was sold off in strips! The Notre-Dame District, now the Jean-Jacques Rousseau District, and the Rue Berbisey have strips of land like this from one end to the other and buildings interlink with each other around minuscule courtyards or by the alleyways known locally as "*traiges*" that disappear deep inside a group of buildings. The Middle Ages had its own typical features such as the pointed gables and the geometrically patterned timbering. The House with the Three Faces has kept an unexpected lookout at the Mirror Corner (Coin du Miroir) in the Rue de la Liberté for the past five hundred years. The house that watched Charles the Bold's triumphant entry into the town in 1474 now stands guard over the flow of buses. On the Place des Halles Champeaux stands the Three Gables House with its three unexpected, dislocated lofts, a style that has provided the inspiration for the modern Bastion de Guise District. In the Rue Verrerie, the overhanging half-timbered houses almost touch each other across the roadway. The Millière House in the Rue de la Chouette

is used as an on-site lesson in architecture for tourist guide books. And beyond the study of architectural styles, there is the story of humanity itself. The heraldic cordon tying together the initials carved on a beam indicate that the owner of the house was a widow. The bronze cat and owl on the roof of another house uphold the mediaeval tradition of symbolism. And you have to keep a careful lookout for such symbols as you wend your way through Dijon's History, marvelling as you do so that you cross the former Chamber of Jewels every day, now the lobby for Dijon's uppercrust, the area between the Palace of the States and Notre-Dame. A design in stone that is overlooked because it is always visible, and which can be seen again on an engraving by Jean Bertholle. Try counting the monsters on the beams, the meat-eating creatures that are half-crocodile and half-dragon which, like the ones on the hospice in Beaune, gobble up the stringers from the Rue Verrerie to the Ruc Amiral Roussin. Look for the carved pillar on which St. Thomas is shown touching Christ's wounds beneath the tree of good and evil; it's at no. 19 Rue Berbisey. Thomas Berbisey had a town house built on this spot and the beauty of the carvings in its courtyard rivalled the work in the courtyard within the Chambellan Mansion. What a long road the family had travelled since the days of Perrenot Berbisey, spice-merchant. Thomas Berbisey was Secretary to Louis XI. And later came Jean Berbisey who, in the 18th century, became the first President of the Parliament! Their tiny emblem, a ewe, comes down to us across four hundred years, in the street that, finally, was given the family's name.

It is difficult to understand Dijon without knowing its family trees. Its great families all develop in the same mould, starting in trade and gaining wealth, and stepping from a position of wealth to power and nobility, displaying their success to the world at large in the street. For, in those days, the streets were like identity cards. Illiteracy will have had the advantage of leaving towns that resembled picture books. Coats-of-arms, shop signs, and voti-

ve statues, the pictograms of an earlier age, can be seen throughout the town, for example Jean Sigault's stork in the Rue Amiral-Roussin, the bunch of grapes in the Rue Monge, the owl on the side of Notre-Dame. Philip the Good himself left his mark on the town (the lighters and flints of the Golden Fleece), in the Ducal Palace.

This is the Dijon of the Great Dukes, and it has many other sights that are a constant source of delight, like the pointed gable on the Law Courts with the swirling rose window, glimpsed between two streets, or the delicate calligraphic stonework whose foliage rolls and unrolls across the door of the Church of Mary Magdalen.

The Renaissance: in the steps of Sambin

Renaissance Dijon shows the profound change in style that accompanied social evolution in the town. The "General Days" held in Beaune had become a regular session of meetings which were then transferred to Dijon where they became the Parliament. The transfer brought the town three hundred years of intense economic, intellectual and artistic activity. Caught between a natural reserve and a desire for ostentation, between their natural tastes and fashion, the gentlemen of the robe commissioned mansions built in a very unusual style. The influence of northern regions was muted here. Everybody swore by the great architectural orders which had been reformulated by an Italy bubbling over with new ideas.

St. Michael's Church in Dijon is an excellent example of the transition between

architectural styles. In the same way, the Law Courts, on which building work began in 1522, has a Gothic attic. Beneath it, the frontage is filled with niches, colonettes, and carvings, all of them decidedly Renaissance in character. The Scrin Doorway, of which the original is in the Art Gallery, was carved by Hugues Sambin. People are rather too quick to say that the profusion of decorative features was the unique hallmark of this outstanding artist who had such a profound effect on Renaissance architecture in Dijon. His

Rue Verrerie is arguably a better place for a quiet stroll.

«signature» is evident in the frontages of mansions such as the Hôtel Lemullier de Bressey in the Rue Chabot Charny, the Lux Mansion on the Place Bossuet, and the Fyot de Mimeure Residence in the Rue Amiral Roussin. All of them have the same semi-circular or triangular pediments, their outlines softened by the same frontage. They have the same pure, austere profiles of women. And the same careworn lions, the eternal spectators of unchanging human vicissitudes.

The residence built in 1561 for Jean Maillard, Mayor of Dijon, is in the same architectural lineage but lacks the masterful composition of the others. It is traditionally attributed to Sambin but is certainly no more than an interpretation of his work. But what matter! The excessiveness and outrageousness of the building has lent fuel to the legend and, in the end, shown the real mastery of a man who did much to elevate his own period in history. And still in his wake comes the House of Caryatids in the Rue Chaudronnerie, a building covered with telamones and caryatids keeping watch at each window on the upper storeys. It is a superb yet, at the same time, clumsy imitation of a temple. The wealthy merchants who commissioned it (the Pouffiers) doubtless wanted a symbol of their social success. Yet true nobility requires no ostentation. The residence built at no. 1 in the same street has no decoration other

The Law Courts,
once the Parliament of Burgundy.

than the rhythmical layout of the rustic bosses and windows with pediments that are carefully structured. It is almost a cube, the walls are rough to the touch, yet it has the amazing appearance of the palaces of Florence, such as the Pitti Palace.

Sambin? He is to be found again in the Rue Vannerie in which the Le Compasseur Mansion has a bartizan that is as ornamented as a mantelpiece in Ecouen. There are terminals above chimera, while lions and grotesque figures are framed in draperies and bunches of fruit. Even the dormer windows on certain buildings unwind stone scrolls decorated with griffons (Rue de la Manutention) with lions (Rue Buffon), or caryatids (Rue des Forges, Rue de la Chouette) and many other buildings are adorned at roof level, so that Sambin is present wherever you look, right up to the skyline! The Renaissance did not just bring with it a whole new vocabulary. It regulated architectural fashion, imposing its own specific rhythm and building material viz. stone. Half-timbered houses, which were a fire hazard, were gradually replaced for security reasons and, also, because they lacked prestige. Dijon, in its use of stone, confirmed the emergence of a new social class.

The upsurge of Classicism

Thanks to its parliamentary nobility, Dijon enjoyed another Golden Age in the 17th and 18th centuries, in both intellectual and architectural terms. Who were its leaders? Crébillon, Piron who crossed literary swords with Voltaire, Lammonoye, Rameau, Bossuet, Buffon who spent his life between Dijon and Montbard, or President de Brosses, whose *Letters from Italy* "are still published today. Dijon attracted all the major architects e.g. Nicolas Lenoir from Paris, Hardouin-Mansart, Gabriel, de Noinville, Jean Caristie from Milan, de Wailly who dared to create the opulence of Montmuzard when it was not itself producing such luxury (the Saint-Père dynasty, Cellerier, Le Muet).

Luxury for the dukes

The dukes of the Valois line were patrons of the arts who lived in great luxury. They rivalled all the great names of the world, commissioning works of art and refurbishing their residences (Dijon, Beaune, Germolles, Rouvres, Aisey, Paris, Arras, Lille, Ghent and Bruges) and their future place of burial (the Carthusian monastery in Champmol). They entertained on a lavish scale.

The dukes' official entries into their «good town» of Dijon remained memor-able occasions. On 23rd January 1474, Charles the Bold, richly attired and covered in gems, crossed the town mounted on a horse caparisoned in cloth of gold and followed by an entire escort to receive the keys of the town, ceremoniously, from the hands of Mayor Etienne Berbisey.

Classical mansions:
8 rue de la Chouette: Vogüé Residence
1 place Saint-Fiacre: small Bohier Residence
12 rue Vauban: Bouhier de Savigny Residence
43-45 rue Chabot-Charny: Barres Residence
1-3 rue Monge: Bouchu Residence
5 rue Berbisey: large Berbisey Residence
27 rue Vauban: Legouz de Gerland Residence
8 place Bossuet: Févret de Saint-Mesmin Residence
39 rue Vannerie: Chartraire de Montigny Residence
47 rue de la Préfecture: Bouhier de Lantenay Residence
40 rue de la Préfecture: Esmonin-Dampierre Residence

All the luxury of Renaissance carving: the Maillard House in Rue des Forges (*top*) and the Caryatid House in Rue Chaudronnerie (*opposite*).

less excessive style. Decorative features were more discreet; architectural expression was evident rather more in the rhythmic layout and forms of windows and in the projections along the frontages.

More than fifty mansions

The Vogüé Residence is the finest of the private mansions in Dijon. Built in 1614 for Etienne Bouhier, Parliamentary Consellor, it was a magnificent example of aristocratic residence set between courtyard and garden, a style that was as highly prized in Dijon as it was in the Marais District in Paris. The superb nature of the building is obvious from the street in the green, gold and black mosaic of its glazed roof tiles. This style of roof, which has been attributed to the influence of Flanders, has become known as a typical feature of Burgundy.

Etienne Bouhier, who was a great patron of the arts, had his house rebuilt after returning from a trip to Italy, and he superimposed the influence of the Renaissance on a Classical style of architecture. This is obvious in the carvings on the bossages of the main entrance, and in the trophies, muzzles, and masks, but it is even more evident in the wonderful portico in the main courtyard. It is built of veined pink stone, carved as delicately as a piece of lacework.

What a sudden, unexpected feeling of exile when, through an expert appraisal of a building, there is a glimmer of a refined civilisation and all the timeless brilliance of Italy is carried into the very heart of a town far away! There are a few magical masterpieces - and the Vogüé Residence is one of them. A building to which the eye never becomes accustomed. It was even selected recently as a film set for *Cyrano de Bergerac*.

Dijon is making every effort to bring this part of its history back to life and give its true worth to these 97 hectares

The Morel-Sauvegrain Residence in Rue des Forges.

During this period, the town took on an appearance that was not to change until the bastions were removed in the late 19th century. And more than one-half of the buildings in the old town centre date from these two centuries. There is no distinct break with the 16th century. Architectural culture used the same language and admired the same models. But it abandoned what the fans of modern architecture then described as "mascarons, ugly tablets, and strange grotesque figures!" Dijon's private townhouses then displayed this new,

The Vogüé Residence,
one of the finest mansions built
in France in the 17th century.

of unique architectural heritage, an area now protected by a preservation order in which there are more than fifty private mansions listed or classified by the Historic Monuments Dept. (the equivalent of the National Trust in Britain). Among the most important, in the Law Courts district, is the tiny Bouhier House in the Rue Vauban built in 1618, and the great Bouhier Mansion built in 1630. Jean Bouhier, who was President of the Parliament, was a brilliant humanist whose library contained no less than 35,000 books and somewhat over 2,000 manuscripts. Beyond it are the Lantin Mansion in the Rue des Bons Enfants (1650-1660) and the Barres Residence in the Rue Chabot-Charny (1650), still with the alternating semi-circular and triangular pediments, and the subtle balance of light and shade regulated by the moulding. The Legouz de la Berchère Residence in the Rue Berbisey, built in 1614, has an entrance decorated with allegories of Justice and Abundance, a veritable open-air frontispiece. Beneath the pediment of the Le Compasseur Mansion is the ample sweep of voussoirs enclosing the two bulls' eye windows in its curves.

Another admirable sense of movement can be seen in the rear vault of the porch on the Blancey Mansion (1660).

The Rue Jeannin contains the Frasans Residence (1621), the Pérard de la Vesvre Mansion (1661) which is remarkable for its Ionic columns above the courtyard, the concise Jehannin de Chamblanc Residence (1673) and the Laloge Residence whose sloping arcades run along the Place Saint-Michel like music played "vibrato". And it is true that the architecture of the 17th century has the same syntax as its music and language. Where you might expect to see the composer Rameau, you will find one of Dijon's authors, Michel Lagrange, who wrote for one of his characters, "Do you not perceive that which unites this architecture and the phrasing of this Great Century? Syntax, choice of words and music..." On the Place des Cordeliers stands the residence built in 1642 for Jean Gauthier, an almost haughty construction with no ornamentation other than simple bossages, like the mansion (1641-1643) that belonged to Jean Bouchu, First President of the Parliament. Its design is ascribed to an architect from Dijon named Pierre Le Muet, better known for his translations of

Dijon in the Classical Era: knowledgeable artists and humanists

The elegant frontages give just a hint of the refinement, erudition and thirst for knowledge of a whole historical period. The parliamentarians not only had mansions built; they also ordered furniture and paintings. They liked reading and music.

Among the best-known local people of the 17th and 18th centuries are artists Philippe Quantin, Bénigne, Gagnereaux, Colson and Jean-Baptiste Lallemant; architect Le Muet; sculptor Jean Dubois; writers Crébillon, Alexis Piron, and Jean Bouhier, Chairman of the Parliament, a booklover with an inquisitive mind who built up one of the largest libraries of the day, President Charles de Brosses whose *Letters from Italy* have become a classic, and, the most famous of all, Jacques-Bénigne Bossuet and Jean-Philippe Rameau.

A house «between courtyard and garden» - an architectural style unique for its refinement and splendour.

Vignola and Palladio. One of these buildings is a quadrangle with a steeply-sloping roof on a narrow strip of land; the other uses a vast expanse of land for a Classical mansion between courtyard and garden, in which the main building between the two wings at right angles uses

the same architectural language without making any concession to the setting. The Bouchu Residence still has its formal garden, with a pond amidst the lawns, a number of bowers and statues, all jealously concealed behind high walls. In 1690, Charles Legouz de Gerland extended the old family home that strings its bartizans out along the Rue Jean-Baptiste Liégeard. Behind it, he commissioned a graceful building with windows underlined by floral bas-reliefs opening onto a semi-circular courtyard, the only copy in Dijon of the Place Royale.

A masterpiece of elegance from the arcades broken up by cascades of flowers to the balustrade toned down by two superb lions and the theatrical entrance with its lion's head mask between the timber drapery. It is said to have been designed by Martin de Noinville, who was also responsible for the delicate Castel Pavilion built c. 1707 for Legouz-Morin. Thus, depending on the land purchased, the mansions clustered together or dispersed, adapting their styles to the setting. Gradually, a subtle change of scale became apparent between the narrow mediaeval streets such as the Rue Verrerie and the streets lined by mansions with taller, more extensive frontages.

What a difference between the first town plan, drawn in 1574 by an artist named Evrard Bresdin and the plan draw between 1756 and 1759 by Mikel, the King's Engineer-Geographer, at the request of the States General and the town council! The first plan is a bird's eye view in which the houses huddle toge-

Top: The Bouhier
de Savigny Residence
in Rue Vauban.

Bottom: The Le Compasseur
de Sassenay Residence
in Rue Berbisey.

ther in close-set rows. Religious buildings and the enclosures of the monastic orders are there, with their gardens. Mikel's plan, the first reliable plan dating back to before the French Revolution, copies the main features. It shows the importance of the religious buildings and the enclosures. But the town has been given fresh air through the laying out of parks and gardens and they provide a certain degree of flexibility by constituting a fund of land for the future. The plan also shows the changes in building habits, by indicating the sites of twenty-three private mansions. All of them are shown as having the same design, built back from the road, between a courtyard and a garden.

At the turn of the century, when the Fevret de Saint-Mesmin Residence was

built on the Place Bossuet, it marked the spread of a new style, with its vast Mansart-style attic. It was built between 1698 and 1700, doubtless to designs supplied by Jules Hardouin-Mansart.

The Rue Vannerie contains a mansion that was altered in 1744-1745 by Marc-Antoine Ier, Charterer of Montigny, and Treasurer General of the States of Burgundy. Its entrance is one of the rare examples of Rococo architecture in Dijon. In fact, its Baroque decoration is so excessive that numerous works on style use the superb flamed shell on its doors as an example of stylistic "excessiveness" in a town that is so very Classical in spirit.

The arrival of Neo-Classicism

Forty years later, in the same mansion, Charles Saint-Père designed a main staircase for Marc-Antoine II in the purest of Neo-Classical styles.

The austere lines of the luxurious residence built in the Rue de la Préfecture between 1756 and 1759 for Bénigne III

Bouhier, Brigadier in the King's Army, confirmed the arrival of Neo-Classical architecture in Dijon. There is an overall impression of horizontality, emphasised by the balustrade concealing the roof. The only particularities are the variations in the windows, the projection with the pediment overlooking the courtyard and garden, and the elegant central building with its cant-walls. The architect, Nicolas

Above: One of the two lions on the balustrade topping the Legouz de Gerland Residence

The elegant semi-circular courtyard in the Legouz de Gerland Residence in Rue Vauban.

A peep inside...

Dijon's conservancy area

The old town centre in Dijon became a conservancy area in 1966 and is one of the most extensive in France, including some three thousand houses from every historical period. The regulations laid down as part of the conservancy and enhancement plan resemble a set of specifications, indicating the work that can be carried out on buildings and the permissible urban improvements. They include mandatory technical conditions relating to upkeep of buildings and obligatory materials and colour schemes, especially for commercial premises, in order to maintain the outstanding architecture in the old streets.

Since 1971, grants are been paid to owners who have made particular efforts in the architectural restoration of their homes or shops in order to encourage the embellishment of the town.

The policies implemented in this respect over more than a quarter of a century have made Dijon particularly popular with the locals and with visitors, thanks to the quality of the urban layout.

Lenoir, familiarly known as "the Roman", altered the small Berbisey Mansion along the same lines (austerity and lack of ornamentation) c. 1761. He was also the architect of the severe but beautiful residence at 34 Rue Buffon and the Pheasantry (now no longer in existence) built in the gardens of Pouilly-les-Dijon for the Marquis Bouhier de Lantenay. Was it the ephemeral nature of things which gives their memory such splendour? It was another, now non-existent masterpiece which marked the general acceptance of Neo-Classicism in Dijon. Claude-Philibert Fyot de la Marche, First President of the Parliament, began laying out the Montmuzard Estate in 1729. The castle, a pure juxtaposition of different volumes, stood in the midst of 74 hectares of gardens and parkland. Set beneath the skies

of Dijon, this building revived the spirit of the Rotunda of Vicence, one of the finest Palladian villas ever built. The castle was demolished in 1795 and the estate was gradually divided up into plots of land. So ended a dream...

Above: A close-up of the Rolin Residence.
Top: A Renaissance dormer window overlooking a concealed courtyard.
Bottom: The measured elegance of the Fyot de Mimeure Residence in Rue Amiral-Roussin.

The frontage of another Neo-Classical building, the Military Headquarters in the Rue Vannerie, is watched over by the gods of war; it was designed by Charles Saint-Père. One of Lenoir's pupils, architect Jacques Cellerier adopted the same austere style for the beautiful Esmonin-Dampierre Mansion in the Rue de la Préfecture. And the architect and contractor, Jean Caristie, who came from Milan, was responsible for the bare yet tastefully elegant frontage of the Richard de Ruffey Mansion (1752) at 33 Rue Berbisey and the residence at 28 Rue Pasteur which he altered for his own family, for it has to be said that although there was a lot of new

building over this century, there was also a fashion for the alteration of existing constructions. Owners added on porticoes and projections, altered windows, had carriage entrances built, gave the porches a more aristocratic air. The last townhouse to be built before the downfall of the monarchy was the Lory Mansion in the Rue Vaillant, built in 1790.

The turning point of the French Revolution

Another long page of history was turned. An entire society collapsed, the society that had built Dijon and swarmed around the delightful castles that were symbols of power and a whole way of life, castles like Vantoux, Beaumont-sur-Vingeanne, Arcelot, Pommard, or Fontaine-Française whose guests included Voltaire, Rousseau, Madame de Staël and Madame Récamier, to name but a few.

Yet the French Revolution in Dijon damaged neither the Palace of States nor civil buildings, with the exception of the Law Courts. Was this an example of intellectual moderation? Probably. But it was also a result of the enclosure of the town within the 12th-century walls, within a space that was so small that it encouraged a total lack of segregation. The private mansions had been built wherever there was a spare plot of land. There were no aristocratic districts and, in this town at least, everybody rubbed shoulders with neighbours, be they noble or lowly, separated only by a courtyard, a garden or a narrow street. Paradoxically, it was the post-Revolutionary period that saw the creation of specific areas or buildings reserved for certain social classes. The upper classes moved out of the old town, leaving an aging centre that has only recently been rediscovered.

Henri Chabeuf, a historian of the Côte-d'Or, wrote of the Dijon of the 1900's, "There's nothing much to say about it. Private and public buildings do

A close-up of the Rolin Residence.

The Bouhier de Lantenay Residence, used by the King's Intendant and today's Chief Regional Administrator.

The military headquarters in Rue Vannerie now house the Regional Department of Cultural Affairs.

The entrance to the military headquarters watched over by gods of war.

more to facilitate social interchange than increase the beauty of the town itself." It is possible to be a little less severe. There are graceful features dating from the Art Nouveau period. There are those who like the Art Deco features or the frontages of villas that are impossible to put into any real category, refugees from a period when seaside resorts were fashionable. The town, though, was no longer built to meet the desires of individuals. It was built to a plan; it met needs. And now, surrounded on all sides, it still escapes us, for the poetry of a town is indefinable. Even if you have read all the guide books and learnt everything there is to know about its history, deciphering all its styles as you go, the town only reveals its true soul very gradually.

This is a town full of symbols, a bestiary-town that should (one might almost say) be discovered by following a cat as it wanders from street to belltower. Enter the town from the south, through the district surrounding the Ouche Gate whose alteration was partly the work of an architect named Nuñez. The Rue Monge still follows the ancient layout of the roads of Antiquity. Take a brief Mediterranean stop near the pond on the Place Emile Zola. The Place Bossuet is more austere and the statue of the famous orator stands, addressing his counterpart, the Perreney de Baleure Mansion that has to

be "read" from close up, from a point at which your gaze, fixed on the front wall, can see the linenfold masks on the pediments, or the grimacing faces surrounding the windows.

Not far away, the Neo-Gothic half-timbering of the Mulot-et-Petitjean House, a gingerbread dowager duchess of a building, looks down over the street. It seems to have been invented by an enthusiastic reader of Hansel and Gretel, concealed behind the pretext of architectural style. And the gnome on the edge of the stringer is still laughing at the joke...

Now for a quick look at the Roofless House, which got its name from a legend and an infamous act. The house was decapitated, like its owner who was accused of using small children as the main ingredient in his pies.. Behind the walls are unbelievable, hidden, secret gardens. Every springtime, a Japanese cherry tree bursts into blossom, as unexpected a sight as the apricot tree nestling in the grounds of the Chamber of Commerce, in the heart of the old cloisters of St. Stephen's.

Take another stroll along the Rue Brulart, an impossible street which is, nevertheless, one of the inevitable routes through Dijon! It resembles the eye of a needle and bears no comparison to the thread of traffic trying to pass through it. It also provides a phenomenal backward glance at history and religious architecture. It has St. John's Church with its tall dark bays (like owls' eyes) behind a frieze of Gothic lacework, then comes the spiny steeple of St. Philibert's and the glazed mitres of St. Bénigne's. Even the Palace of States marks out the road, running up the Rue Berbisey until it meets the ox that juts out from the wall on the Place Jean-Macé, caught in the act of escaping over the wall, an act that has now lasted for hundreds of years. From there, the Rue du Bourg resembles a delicate pastry puff of shops, far removed from its sinister past when it was the shambles, in the days when the R. Suzon flowed through it, open to the sky. Cutting off the view at the end are the golden

Place de la Libération, enclosed by buildings on all sides, was once a military parade ground.

and green ornamentations of the Aubriot Residence, one of the key views in the town. The brilliant scales of the glazed tiles are encased within the reddish-brown of the roofs.

Leaving the shops behind you, you will cross the last outer ring of the hill-fort, the almost intangible trace that circles the Palace, an area that seems to summarise the entire town, in streets that twist and turn or form sudden, unexpected successions of thoroughfares. The light plays on the pediments above the windows, clambers across the cornices, sparkles on the scrolls round the dormer windows, casts a shade around a barti-zan or a row of balustrades, and gives a grave or cynical appearance to the many faces carved on the buildings in the town, for it has to said that few of the masks show a smile. Visitors to Dijon always feel the reserve that characterises the house-fronts, and the local people.

And what is the highlight of a visit? The arrival in the centre of the town, a place worthy of an expert in strategy or a great film director. On the Place de la Libération, where the town plays out its great majestic, Classical drama every day, the Terrace Tower casts an ever-quizzical eye on the surrounding grandeur.

From the top, you can at last see the entire town. It is an artist's palette full of copper tones, browns and greys against a background of stone, with touches of green. Encircled in mist, a golden conden-sation in the sunset and a blue-tinted veil early in the morning. Sometimes, it is a chromatic picture like the works by Vieira da Silva in the town's Art Gallery; some-times, a miniature from a Book of Hours, with its walled gardens, and noble, pre-cise architecture.

This is an infinitely beautiful town which gets its charm from the past and from the wit and wisdom of those who bring it to life.

GRAINETERIE

The art of shop signs

Since 1984, Dijon Town Council has been encouraging the creation of qua-lity shop signs in the old town centre by awarding special grants.
Shop signs are streetwise illustrations of trades, wares or crafts, some of them picturesque and others more straightforward. They require talent on the part of designers, wrought irons-miths, painters or even master glass painters. They contribute to the user-friendly atmosphere in streets such as Rue Amiral-Roussin, Rue Verrerie or Rue Musette.

From a fresco in the covered market to the weepers on the Dukes' tomb - variations in artistic expression and differing historical periods.

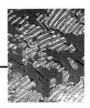

THE TREASURE TROVE IN THE MUSEUMS

Dijon is not an open-air museum but it has many museums with extensive collections that make it an influential cultural and artistic centre.

Dijon's museums and art galleries have undergone major modernisation and development over the past twenty years.

But let's give honour where honour's due! **The Art Gallery** (*Musée des Beaux-Arts, on the Place de la Sainte Chapelle*) is without doubt one of France's foremost museums, because of its age (it was first opened in 1787 by the members of the Elected body that administered Burgundy in pre-Revolutionary days), its setting in the Palace of States, and the sheer size of its collections. Once famous for its collection of works by Flemish and Burgundian primitives and for the tombs of the Dukes of Burgundy, it has recently extended its Modern and Contemporary Art section thanks to the Granville donation.

The riches handed down by the Dukes of Burgundy are exhibited in chambers that were once part of their palace. The **Sainte-Chapelle Chapter House** is in the Bar Tower (built in the second half of the 14th century), and includes a collection of items concerned mainly with the Order of the Golden Fleece created in 1430 by Philip the Good, which had its seat in the Sainte-Chapelle. There are a number of carvings showing the artistry of the successors of Claus Sluter, Claus de Werve and Juan de La Huerta. The chamber containing the ducal tombs, which was given the name of **Guardroom** in the 17th century, also serves as a reminder of the Gothic palace. It was Philip the Good's "reception room". The Flamboyant Gothic fireplace, which was altered and renovated in 1827 and 1898, was carved by John of Angers.

Since 1827, this magnificent chamber has housed the tombs and altar screens from the old Carthusian monastery in Champmol which was closed during the French Revolution and demolished a few years later. The **tomb of Philip the Bold,**

Top: Scenes from days gone by in the Museum of Burgundian Life.

Bottom: An unexpected sight in the Granville Collection, Buri's *Cow-Landscape*.

The Nativity by the Master of Flémolle is one of the most outstanding examples of Flemish art. It can be seen in the Art Gallery.

The Guardroom in the Museum of Fine Arts contains the tomb of Philip the Bold, watched over for eternity by lions and gilded angels.

which was commissioned by the Duke himself in 1381 (he died in 1404), was carved by Flemish sculptors i.e. Jean de Marville (the black marble mausoleum), Claus Sluter (the designs for the "weepers" and the carving of some of the figures), and Claus de Werve (most of the "weepers", the recumbent statue, the angels and the lion). It was not completed until 1410. The upper section was partially rebuilt during the 19th century, but the silent procession of monks, the variety of attitudes, and the marked feeling of prayer and meditation make this masterpiece a rare example of mediaeval carving at its very best. The **tomb of John the Fearless and Margaret of Bavaria** was inspired by the same design. Commissioned in 1443 by Philip the Good, John the Fearless' son, it was carved by a sculptor from Aragon named Juan de La Huerta and a sculptor from Avignon, Antoine Le Moiturier. It was completed in 1470. The style of this second tomb is more akin to Flamboyant Gothic, but it is quite acceptable to state a preference for the more deeply realistic work by Claus Sluter. Also from Champmol is the **Crucifixion Reredos** (1393), a wonderful piece of

work by Jacques de Baerze and, for the gold leaf and paintings on the rear of the shutters, Melchior Broerderlam (1399). Another altar screen was carved by Jacques de Baerze and a workshop in Angers. The chamber also houses the *Portrait of Philip the Good* painted in the workshop of Roger Van der Weyden (1445).

The numerous Flemish **primitives** flank the admirable *Nativity* by the Master of Flémalle, Robert Campin (1420). This is an important example of Flemish painting in the period between Broederlam and Van Eyck. In addition to works by Thierry Bouts, Van der Weyden's school etc. are Italian, Swiss, German and Spanish primitives, illustrating late mediaeval art throughout Europe.

The 18th century is well represented. Then comes the model of the *Departure of the Volunteers* (better-known as *The Marseillaise*), carved by François Rude for the Arc de Triomphe in Paris. Beyond it is a room dedicated to the works of François Pompon etc. There are works by Italian, Flemish, and Dutch artists, in all more than 20,000 sketches and 80,000 engravings.

And now to the Granville Bequest. Some of the works that form a counterpoint are old, such as Georges de La Tour's *Glassblower by lamplight* (17th century). The 19th century is represented by Eugène Delacroix, Théodore Géricault, Victor Hugo, the artists of the Barbizan School, Jean-François Millet, Gustave Courbet etc. The contemporary and modern art collection draws on works by Rouault, Braque, Juan Gris, Kandinsky, Matisse and friends of Pierre Granville such as Bertholle, Hajdu, Manessier, Szenes, or Vieira da Silva. Charles Lapicque has an entire room to himself. A few yards away are four of the famous *Footballers* by Nicolas de Staël.

Once upon a time, there were... two enlightened, sensitive art lovers named Maurice and Jeanne Magnin. Brother and sister. He was a Counsellor at the Audit Office; she was an art critic and painter. They lived in the fine mansion built in the mid 15th century for Etienne Lantin, Master Counsellor at Dijon's Chamber of Accounts. In 1938, having no direct heirs, they gifted the mansion and the collections in it to the State. This is the wonderful

The weepers on the tomb of Philip the Bold.

A close-up of the door to the Law Courts, carved by Hugues Sambin. It is now kept in the Museum of Fine Arts.

Magnin Museum (4 rue des Bons Enfants) which has retained, unspoilt, the atmosphere of a private home in which art was held in the very highest esteem.

In the shadow of St. Bénigne's, in the main wing of the former Benedictine Abbey which was closed down during the French Revolution, is the **Archaeological Museum** (5 Rue du Docteur Maret). Since 1955, it has been housed in the old Romanesque-style chapter house, now in the basement (early 11th century, when William of Volpiano commissioned the rebuilding of the abbey), the former monks' dorter (a 13th-century Gothic chamber with wide windows dating from the 17th century) and the rooms above, used as the monks' cells (17th century).

The basement houses the Gallo-Roman collections of archaeological exhibits. Among them are fascinating items from the **sanctuary at the source of the R. Seine** (some 18 miles from Dijon). The site has been subject to archaeological digs for over one hundred years and has revealed several remarkable pieces such as the **Goddess Sequana on her boat** (a bronze carving). It was approximately thirty years ago that Roland Martin and Simone Deyts made their extraordinary discovery of over one thousand **votive offerings** piled up in a sculptor's workshop (bronzes, stone and, mostly, wooden items).

On the ground floor are Romanesque tympani (from St. Bénigne's dating from the 12th century, entitled **The Last Supper** and **Christ in Glory**). There are also capitals from St. Philibert's, carvings by Claus Sluter and his school (a **bust of Christ** designed for the calvary of the church in Champmol in 1400, and a statue of **Christ on the Cros**s by Claus de Werve).

The most elderly of all the people of Burgundy, **Genay man** (dating from 70,000 B.C.), keeps watch over the remains of the Paleolithic Age on the first floor. The **Blanot Treasure** which is shown off to its full advantage, and the **golden bracelet of La Rochepot**, which was recently unearthed by chance, are an excellent illustration of the Late Stone Age. The collection also includes some wonderful little bronze figures of Mâlain, the mother goddesses of Alesia and the god of Chorey, representing the Roman period.

Built between 1699 and 1708 for Cistercian nuns from Notre-Dame de Tart, who had lived in Dijon since the 17th century, and based on the layout of the Benedictine church in Val-de-Grâce in Paris, St. Anne's Church was no longer used during the Revolution and it became a storehouse for religious artefacts. Left unused for many years, it was given a new lease of life in 1979 when it became the **Museum of Sacred Art** (15 Rue Sainte-Anne). Thanks to its founder, canon Jean Marilier, it has saved and shown off to their full advantage masterpieces from various churches in the Côte-d'Or. All that remains of the original church is the wrought-iron screen in the chancel, made by a craftsman from Dijon named Pichot. The High Altar not only has its place within the history of sculpture (a unique piece of work dated

c. 1670 by a great sculptor from Dijon named Jean Dubois) but, having been brought here from the Chapel of the Visitation which was demolished during the French Revolution, it serves as a reminder of the first Mass celebrated anywhere in the world in honour of the Sacred Heart, on 4th February 1689. It illustrates the Visitation of the Virgin Mary to St. Elizabeth.

Next to this museum, and also part of the former Cistercian convent, is the **Perrin-du-Puycousin Museum of Burgundian Life** (17 Rue Sainte-Anne) which has been housed in the cloisters since 1982. Maurice Perrin du Puycousin (1856-1949) was a barrister in Tournus, with a passion for the folk-lore of Burgundy and Bresse at a time where he was considered to be a pioneer in his field. He opened a magnificent museum in Tournus in 1929. The remainder of his collections went to Dijon where he set up a second museum in 1938. This museum, the result of a lifelong passion, was created by Madeleine Blondel. It was then closed and, later, restructured. It now presents the stages of life, the crafts, cookery, and family furniture common to rural Burgundy. In addition, there are old shops laid out in an imaginary Dijon street, each shop having been saved in its entirety over the past few years. A way of paying homage to local food industries e.g. blackcurrant liqueur, mustard, spice bread, biscuits etc.

The pavilions built in the early years of the 17th century for the Knights of the Arquebuse now house the **Museum of Natural History** (1 avenue Albert Ier) which has been reorganised and skilfully restored over the past few years. The ground floor houses the regional geology exhibition that casts an eye outward to distant horizons. It has a skeleton of an ichtyosaur brought here from the Wurtemburg region and a fossilised

The Footballers by Nicolas de Staël, one of the masterpieces in the Granville Bequest.

Below: St. Paul (Museum of Sacred Art).

glyptodont from the pampas of Argentina. The regional ecology rooms are on the first floor where entire Burgundian landscapes have been recreated. The second floor is the insect kingdom. At the end of the garden stands the **Orangery** which houses temporary exhibitions, a reptile house and even a beehive used as a teaching aid.

The passion of two lives

Pierre Granville and his American wife, Kathleen, both of whom are now dead, were art enthusiasts. So much so, in fact, that they left the theatre and the cinema in 1948 to devote themselves to their overriding passion, modern and contemporary painting and sculpture. Writing under the pen-name Chantelou, Pierre Granville covered art auctions for the newspaper, Le Monde. He published articles in leading art journals. Their friends included Vieira da Silva, Arpad Szenes, Etienne Hadju, Charles Lapicque, Jean Bertholle and Manessier and they played a major part in launching the young Nicolas de Staël.

In their small Parisian apartment, hundreds of works of art filled all available space. Many of the works were gifts, since the couple had no personal fortune. They decided to bequeath their collection to a museum, because they were childless, and thought of Dijon's Musée des Beaux-Arts which had only a fairly limited collection of works illustrating these artistic trends at that time. In 1969, the museum was restructured to make way for the Granville Bequest, a reminder of a passion that had filled two lives. Given the current lack of space, it would perhaps be appropriate to reconsider the presentation of contemporary art in Dijon, especially as there are now extensive collections, especially of conceptual art, with the F.R.A.C. and the Consortium.

Top: Etienne Hajdu's
The work of the Wind
in the Clemenceau Garden.

Bottom: The grounds
surrounding the Château de Larrey.

THE "YELLOW JERSEY" OF GREEN TOWNS

The "Little Gardener" is one of the most popular characters in Dijon.
And meeting him is no problem at all.
Just go to the Rue des Forges and up the stairs in the Chambellan Residence.
You'll find him right at the very top.

His basket is brimful of exotic fronds that stretch up to the vaulting, intertwine with it, and change into flamboyant architectural motifs. The locals have always had green fingers in this town.

Dijon has 600 hectares of gardens and public parks. Whether old or new, its open spaces tell the tale of gardens from the Middle Ages onwards. The botanic gardens are world famous and the Gloire de Dijon, which was created in 1853 by Jacotot, unfolds its yellow-tinted pinkish beige petals in any modern catalogue of old roses. Every three years (1996, 1999 etc.) the **Florissimo Exhibition** attracts more than 150,000 visitors to Burgundy's capital.

Two majestic pillars topped with garlanded vases (1672), the remains of one of Dijon's old town gates, now lead to the **Cours du Parc**, of which the first section now bears the name of General de Gaulle. "The most beautiful avenue in France", wrote the intendant (the "Prefect" in pre-Revolutionary France), quite justifiably, to the Prince de Condé, Governor of the Province. It is very wide and is almost one mile long and it is totally devoid of curves. "It's as curly as the paths in the Parc" was a traditional saying in Dijon when describing hair that remained despairingly straight. Laid out in 1771 by the Town Council, with the assistance of the Intendant, the Parc is an avenue of lime trees set out in the fashion of the day. The roundabout halfway between the Place Wilson and the Colombière dates from 1868. The Memorial to those who died in the First World War replaced a plain pond in 1924. The neighbouring esplanade, reserved for

The Bear in the Darcy Garden, in honour of sculptor François Pompon.

outdoor entertainments (le Carrousel), has become a water sports stadium.

The walled **Parc de la Colombière** extends over 34 hectares to the R. Ouche, which separates it from the Castel de la Colombière (now a riding centre). The central avenue leads the eye along to the Castel at the end. The park was laid out in the 17th century by Louis II de Bourbon, Prince de Condé, Governor of Burgundy. In 1675-1685, his son, Henri-Jules, Duke d'Enghien, commissioned the building of the small chateau and had the park landscaped and planted. Le Nôtre seems to have provided inspiration for the layout. He sent one of his best pupils, Antoine de

Maerle, to Dijon for this purpose. It is a formal park, and is highy representative of the work of the great landscape gardener with decorative flowerbeds along the river bank and avenues and paths radiating outwards to form a star. There are many different species of trees in the park, which is open to the public. Confiscated during the French Revolution and designated as "national property", it was purchased by the town in 1800. There was some talk of turning it into a hippodrome - hence the circular avenue that still exists today.

The Temple of Love (17th century) comes from the castle of Bierre-lès-Semur. The Colombière also contains a fragment of the so-called "Agrippine Way". In his tales of his travels through France in 1877 (*A Little Tour in France*), Henry James described, on the very last page, his amazement at the sight of this park. "A place in which everything falls into place".

With its 3,500 species of plants in 66 beds bordered by low-cut box hedges, the Arquebuse (Avenue Albert Ier) is one of the richest botanic gardens in the world. Its library, herb collections (more than 200,000 plants), and its catalogue which is published annually in Latin before being sent to all four corners of the globe, bear witness to a deep-rooted scientific tradition. Georges Leclerc de Buffon was, after all, a Burgundian. The former exercise yard of the Knights of the Arquebuse has belonged to the municipality since 1808. Originally created in 1771 by Bénigne Legouz de Gerland on another site, the botanic gardens were transferred here in 1833. The botany school contains most of Burgundy's indigenous plants, a large number of French plants, and various strange or tropical species. There is also an arboretum (its *Cedrela chinensis* is believed to be the oldest specimen of its kind in France) and a park. Here, as in La Colombière, Love has its temple; the one in these gardens comes from the chateau at Bessey-lès-Cîteaux.

The *Gloire de Dijon* rose and the Arquebuse Gaden..

The **Darcy Garden** (Place Darcy) dates from the 19th century and is a good example of the vigorous, unemotional town planning of the day. It is also an attractive layout of an underground reservoir in the centre of the town, making skilful use of the break in levels. There is symmetry along the axis of the William Gate (porte Guillaume) but there is also a blend of intimacy and majesty that is tinged with surrealism thanks to the presence of François Pompon's White Bear (or rather, the replica by the sculptor's friend Martinet of a work that brought fame to the sculptor from Burgundy at the Autumn Salon in 1922). Terraces, balustrades, waterfalls, flights of steps and small lakes underline the Italianate style that was so popular in the days of Napoleon III. The gardens designed by Félix Vionnois were also novel for their ornamentation, beds filled with brightly-coloured flowers, a feature that was almost impossible before greenhouses came into use. The Neo-Renaissance monument above the reservoir (1840) is topped by a bust of Henry Darcy carved by Jouffroy in homage to the hydraulics engineer who gave Dijon not only its railway but also its running water.

The 19th century brought the town several other gardens. Behind the Palace of States is the **Square des Ducs** which stands on the site of the erstwhile garden of Margaret of Flanders, wife of Philip the Bold. It is said that a porpoise from Holland once splashed and played in the waters here. Deer and wild boar could be seen there in the 18th century. Redesigned in 1863, the small garden, which is decorated with a statue of Philip the Good by Henry Bouchard and with a few archaeological remains, is a wonderful example of what can be done with the minimum of space.

The **Parc du Château de Larrey** (on the Avenue Eiffel and Boulevard Marmont) has retained all the charm of a late 19th-century upper-class residence with its grotto and small rockery bridge, and its artificial waterfall. The park was sold to the town council by the Jeu family in 1980 and has been open to the public since 1982. As to the **Square Carrelet de Loisy** (Rue Buffon and Rue Legouz Gerland), which was purchased by the council in 1972 and opened to the public a year later, it is reminiscent of English gardens. It stands on the site of the old bakehouse near St. Stephen's Abbey. The **Parc des Argentières** (Rue des Petites Roches and Rue Charles Royer), like the previous two examples, illustrates the policy of providing the town with open spaces based on the acquisition of private gardens, rather than letting the land be sold off for property development. The avenue of lime trees, the orchard and the pathways running secretively between the box hedges still have all the delights of a family garden, once the property of the d'Arbaumonts (Les Argentières is a large estate that has existed for several hundred years).

The statue of Philip the Good in Square des Ducs.

The ponds in the Darcy Garden.

Inaugurated in 1964, the **Canon-Kir Lake** is one of those works which required patience and miracles that can only be wrought by an obstinate desire to succeed. Rather like a three-masted schooner placed in a bottle! Everybody in Dijon contested this fad on the part of Canon Kir. A lake, they said, would attract mosquitoes, it would be overgrown with rushes, it would cost too much to build etc. But the thing was that Canon Kir, who was elected Mayor and M.P. for Dijon in 1945, at the age of 69, was an old country priest and he did not need the services of a sociologist to know all about the local character. Nor did he need a public enquiry to find out what was missing in Dijon; it was water. A town with no water is a town without dreams. There were those who suggested a swimming pool. The Canon retorted ironically that his colleagues wanted to impose "a footbath". No, he had his own idea on the subject, an idea that he presented to the Council meeting in 1945 the first time he himself attended it. What Dijon needed was a lake!

The Meeting shrugged its shoulders. Building was one thing, but undertaking a major landscaping project at his age!

Top: The Château de Larrey park.

Bottom: Lake Kir, a favourite destination for locals seeking a place to relax and have a stroll.

The Town Council believed that this recently-elected councillor, at the age of 69, would not be standing for re-election. In fact, he remained Mayor of Dijon for twenty-two years. With one idea firmly anchored in his mind, to create his lake. Why? Oh, the answer was simple, one might say. When he was attending the seminary in Plombières-les-Dijon in 1895, Félix Kir was enchanted by an idea put forward by one of his teachers. The R. Ouche often flooded the fields and

meadows between Plombières and Dijon; why not dam the river and make an artificial lake which would make the countryside much more attractive. Canon Kir was to remember this idea half a century later. Forcing nature to do as he wanted and create the geographical layout he had determined, was in his character. The idea met with unanimous hostility but he was undaunted. "Who is in favour?" the Mayor-M.P. asked the Council. Nobody replied, except himself. "Motion passed" he concluded, amidst gales of laughter.

The lake is delightful, especially since the 30 hectares round about have been redesigned and landscaped. A small monument by Jacques Yencesse (1976) serves as a reminder of the hard-headed Mayor. And since 1970, *The Grenadier*, a statue by a local sculptor, Georges Diéboit (who also carved *The Zouave*), which was originally to be seen on the Alma Bridge in Paris, has been standing to attention on the edge of the RN 5 road.

Near the lake and the Fontaine d'Ouche, there is **Parc de la Combe-à-la-Serpent**, which was laid out at the same time as the lake. The one million cubic metres of rubble removed to form the lake provided the foundations for the football pitches on this site. It was laid out in the 1970's and consists of 326 hectares landscaped by Bernard Gulepa and André Holodynski. In days gone by, the grass snake was known as "a serpent" and it is not an uncommon sight among the stones. But the "serpent" is also a heraldic figure mentioned in folk tales. Henri Vincenot describes his walks through the combe in his schooldays in his book *La Billebaude*. And just what is a "combe" in Burgundian terms? A dry valley rising from the Saône Plain up to the plateau, like the blind valleys in the Jura. A narrow gorge wending its way between rocks, box wood, twisted oaks, and scree. As you leave the Fontaine d'Ouche district, you can see the Town of Dijon vineyards on your

left. They were replanted in 1981 on the site of the Marcs-d'Or ducal enclosure, and they produce an excellent white Burgundy (Chardonnay) for the cellars of the Town Council and its tenant farmer. Beyond the vineyards is the traditional combe landscape. One side is covered with trees and copses; the other is more arid. The vegetation corresponds to the warm and cold sides of the valley. More than 70 hectares are still farmed. The Dijon Observatory lies right at the head of the combe in La Serpent, on the plateau.

The **Parc de la Combe-Saint-Joseph**, between the town and the Bergerie to which generations of local people have gone "for a breath of fresh air" and a chance to think, covers 15 hectares around the Billenois spring. Laid out in 1982 by André Holodynski and Jacques Dolveck, it is a wonderful evocation of "the state of nature" and both flora and fauna have been carefully preserved. This is an excellent place in which to learn about the natural environment of Dijon. A third combe, the **Parc de la Combe-Persil**, is soon to be laid out to complete this area of open spaces, providing protection for the entire southwestern corner of Dijon.

The **Parc des Carrières-Bacquin** (Rue des Marmouzots) is frequently quoted as an excellent example of the re-use of old quarry sites. For centuries, it provided "Dijon stone", which was used to build houses and monuments. The quarry had ceased functioning some seventy years before the Council bought over its 5 hectares, in 1971. A poetic use of the bulldozer by André Holodynski turned it into an extraordinary garden (1974-1976). Relandscaped, given an artificial waterfall, the geographical features of the old quarry are a never-ending source of surprises for visitors with the rock garden, open-air theatre, flower-filled terrace, romantic lake etc.

Is that all? No. The Canal Harbour (Place du 1er Mai) has also been touched by the magic wand. Laid out in the late

Gardens recreated in the heart of the town

In towns and cities, courtyards and car parks often replace old gardens. Dijon, however, has worked to recreate the original purpose of certain areas.

In the heart of the old town, for example, when the Sainte-Anne car park was built in 1984, the garden was also recreated and divided into four box-lined flowerbeds. This was originally the garden of the Carmelite cloisters, the convent buildings dating from the 17th century now being used by the Greater Dijon District offices.

Not far away, the old gardens in the former convent of the Bernardine Order were laid out in 1623 within the walls of what is now the Museum of Burgundian Life and the Museum of Sacred Art. They have been partially preserved - the old vegetable garden and orchard have been grassed over and planted with lime trees and planes for shade.

The small garden which, in the 18th century, lay beyond the mansion built for Claude Philibert Fyot de la Marche and which opens onto rue Sainte-Anne, has been bought by the Town Council and been recreated as it once was.

18th century on the Burgundy Canal, **the harbour** fulfilled an economic and industrial purpose for many years. In 1977, the harbour facilities were transferred to Longvic. The old harbour then took on a new lease of life as a mooring for river cruisers and yachts. The lake covers 3 hectares. In its centre is an island that has remained inaccessible to visitors in order to ensure that the birdlife has a quiet place in which to nest and live. The surrounding open spaces cover a total of 4 hectares (1979-1984). Wonderful vegetation surrounds the obelisk (or to be more precise, the pyramid) erected in 1786 by Emiland Gauthey to commemorate the linking of all the seas by the new canal. As to the **Winged Dream** by

a light infantryman from the Mont-Blanc area. There were a number of bloody skirmishes in Dijon during the Franco-Prussian War of 1870. The **Clemenceau Gardens** (Boulevard Clemenceau, Rue André Malraux) in the heart of the renovated urban district near the music academy contains a sculpture by Etienne Hajdu named *The Work of the Wind*. The **Parc des Grésilles** (Rue Castelnau), which was inaugurated in 1987, stretches over 3 hectares and was landscaped by André Holodynski. The **Promenade de l'Ouche** was completed in 1986. Its 2,200 metres of footpaths run from the general hospital to the Canon Kir lake, along the banks of a river that was slow-

The canal harbour was refurbished a few years ago to cater for pleasure cruisers.

the Burgundian sculptor Robert Rigot (1981), it serves as a useful reminder of the fact that Gustave Eiffel was born just across the water on the Quai Nicolas Rolin, on 15th December 1832. His mother ran a coal depot in the harbour.

Among recent developments are the **Parc du Drapeau** (literally "Flag Park", in the Avenue du Drapeau, Avenue du Général Fauconnet) laid out in 1981. Which flag? The colours of the 61st Pomeranian Regiment which were captured from the enemy on this spot on 23rd January 1871 by Victor Curtat,

ly but surely "reacquired". This first stage will be completed by others until the path finally extends from the Place du 1er Mai to the Parc de la Colombière. A whole multitude of small plots of land are being patiently turned over to public ownership so that they can eventually form a "swathe of green". There is also the **Promenade du Ruisseau-de-la-Fontaine-d'Ouche** (at the corner of the Boulevard Chanoine-Kir and the Boulevard Gaston-Bachelard, but it can also be reached from the Gorgets viaduct). It is filled with ash, Italian

poplars, alders, and one hundred and one willows, almost all of them centenarians. The Promenade has been created out of a spring, the Ouche, which probably provided the inspiration for the song entitled *Sur la route de Dijon*. It includes the lines, "There was a spring, a spring to which the birds flocked.."

The Rigoley de Chevigny Residence, a folly and an amazing "secret garden" in the heart of the town.

Calves kidneys
in Chablis and
mustard sauce.

Photo by Didier Benaouda.

THE ART OF BEING A HEALTHY TRENCHERMAN

Which room are you shown into when you visit people in Dijon?
The kitchen, of course. First and foremost to the ducal kitchens,
now used by the town council as a reception chamber for most of its guests.

The town might have a well-established reputation for gourmet cooking but it used to lack advertising genius and the image provided by public relations. The Mayor of Dijon during the interwar years, Gaston Gérard, launched the **Good Food Fair** in 1921 and it has remained a major event in anybody's diary for November, with its famous **Lucullus' Table**. The untiring Gaston Gérard also created the Commandery of Cordon Bleu Chefs of France and summoned the States General of French Gourmet Food every year. For hours on end, those in attendance discuss the best diameter for the grains of salt that are sprinkled on the stewed veal with carrots or whether or not the cock used in the *Coq au Chambertin* should be a virgin. Among the ageless recommendations of these wise men of the kitchen are the pinning of the serviette across one's chest or the use of a gravy spoon.

Gaston Gérard strengthened the image of Dijon as a centre of culinary excellence throughout the 1920's and 30's. The finest dishes of all are the saddle of hare à la Piron, the Dijon broach supreme from Racouchot, Dijon asparagus, marbled Easter ham, snails, eggs poached in red wine, coq au vin and the "Belle Dijonnaise" pear dessert, with blackcur-

rant liqueur of course. After loosening its grip on the culinary world for a short time, the "nouvelle cuisine", or new style of cookery, has re-awakened local enthusiasm, although, needless to say, it has been adapted to the local temperament which would not appreciate a half-empty plate. In Dijon, people prefer to have something to get their teeth into. Regional cooking reconciles adepts of every culinary fashion, especially as it is the style of cookery that has been practised in Burgundy since time immemorial. Jean-Pierre Billoux has come from Digoin to breathe life into this style of cuisine while Jean-Paul Thibert is progressing rapidly along the road to stardom.

By offering "Baby Jesus" the traditional Burgundian Christmas gifts of a bottle of blackcurrant liqueur, a slab of spice bread, and a pot of mustard, the Three Kings fill His cradle with presents that are much more precious than gold, frankincense and myrrh. For Dijon, these three products are like a tricolour, with three different flavours and three different aromas.

Cheese puffs.
Photo by Didier Benaouda.

Chicken à la Gaston-Gérard

One day, Curnonsky paid a call on Gaston Gérard, Mayor of Dijon. His wife had intended to serve chicken cooked in white wine with Comté cheese. By mistake, she dropped the box of paprika into the saucepan so, to remedy the situation, she added some fresh cream. Curnonsky, the «Prince of Good Food» found it delicious - and a new recipe was born in Dijon, Chicken à la Gaston-Gérard.

61

The European Centre for the Science of Taste and Dietary Behaviour

It was in 1977 that the European Centre for the Science of Taste and Dietary Behaviour opened its doors. It is an institute, a foundation, and a technology transfer centre, set up by the *Centre national de la recherche scientifique* (CNRS, national centre for scientific research) with several partners including the university, the Regional Council, the Dijon District Council, the Danone Group etc.

This made Dijon one of the main centres of research into human diet in Europe, backed up by the opening of the national institute of agronomical research within the research centre specialising in the value of food as a factor in health (scheduled to open in 1998), the Jules-Guyot vine and wine institute, the national college of biology applied to nutrition and food etc.

They also mark three traits of the local character i.e. gentleness, firmness, and piquancy. Or the heart, soul and mind, if you prefer. The snails created in the 1930's by master chocolate maker Robert Cretton and publicised by Salvador Dali in a well-known advert ("I'm crazy about Lanvin chocolates!") is a traditional local sweet, like the blackcurrant "cassissines" invented in 1910 by the Duthu chocolate factory and the Breuil family, or the "jacquelines", "gimblettes" and many other confectionary delights. The Jeannenez cakeshop began marketing a chocolate owl in 1988.

Dijon mustard, which has been famous since the 14th century, is produced by crushing black or brown mustard seeds after sifting or sieving before leaving them to macerate in verjuice, without the addition of any other herbs or spices. The verjuice is either a green wine obtained by pressing grapes that are not fully ripe, or a bitter wine. Locals used to grow a type of grape especially for this purpose, called "Bordelais" of course as a jibe at the other main wine-producing area! But its culture died out as a result of the phylloxera epidemic and producers now use low-quality white wines. As to mustard flour, it is imported mainly from Canada.

Mustard was first mentioned in the archives in 1336, on the occasion of a ducal banquet held in Rouvres. After that, it cropped up time and time again. Unfortunately, the name "Dijon mustard" is not protected by a trademark and it is made throughout the world. Yet the label has added to the fame of Dijon which still provides most of France's mustard, condiments and sauces under the brand names Amora,

Maille, Grey-Poupon, Parizot, Bornier etc. In all, approximately 45,000 tonnes a year. "Old-style mustard" (moutarde à l'ancienne) is a non-sifted mustard containing whole mustard seeds.

The raw material for **Dijon blackcurrant** (*cassis de Dijon*) comes from blackcurrant bushes grown mainly in the Hautes-Côtes area. The fruit is used to produce liqueurs, syrup or cordials, and forms the basis of a thousand and one popular recipes that make use of the leaves, fruit, buds and bark. In 1840, two liqueur manufacturers from Dijon who were passing through Paris were struck by the fashion for blackcurrant in the French capital and realised that there was a market for their products. In 1855, Pierre Lhéritier married Claudine Guyot. In 1858, Elizabeth Lagoute and Henri Lejay were wed in their turn. This marked the creation of the Lejay-Lagoute and Lhéritier-Guyot companies which with Boudier and several others, are still keeping tradition alive. By a ruling handed down by the Supreme Court of Appeal in France (*Cour de Cassation*) in 1925, manufacturers of blackcurrant-based products bearing the name "Dijon" must have their premises within the town itself. Yet although this is a flourishing sector, with an output of 120,000 hectolitres per year, representing one-half of the 10,000,000 bottles sold annually, its success is based largely on the success of **kir**, a blackcurrant cocktail.

The blackcurrants are crushed and left to macerate in alcohol for several weeks. Sugar is then added and the liquid is mixed. Crème de cassis has a minimum alcohol content of 16°; liqueur is nearer 20°. Blackcurrant products are widely used in cooking and cake making in Dijon. You might like to try calves liver fried with blackcurrant berries or a vacherin, a meringue and ice cream dessert with blackcurrants.

Who first had the idea of blending one-third, or a little less, Crème de cassis with Aligoté wine from the Hautes-Côtes, a dry white wine with a lot of body? Every family in Dijon has its own version of an invention that would seem to have been created by mere chance. There are those who say that a customer in a bar ordered a vermouth and blackcurrant and that the barman took down a bottle of Aligoté by mistake. Whatever the true story, the aperitif was being served in the town hall as early as 1905 when it was called a "young lady" (pucelle). In 1945, when the new M.P. and Mayor, Canon Kir, revived the old tradition, it gradually became universally known and people spontaneously began to talk about a "kir". Nowadays, wherever you are in the world, this short word which was included in the Petit Larousse dictionary as a common noun in 1976 (only eight years after the canon's death) can be found on many a restaurant wine list. If served with red wine, it is known as a Khrushchev, a "communard" etc. Served with a sparkling wine such as the Crémant de Bourgogne, it becomes a "kir royal". Any other way of serving it is sheer heresy...

It is said that Genghis Khan's cavalry received spice bread in their rations. From Dijon? It's highly unlikely but it was almost certainly as hard and unyielding as the "cake" sold here. It is rock hard, a "slab of good health" that is difficult to bite through but that melts on the tongue. There is no connection between this delicacy and the sickly sweet, synthetic sponge that is often sold under the same name. Made with rye flour, honey and spices, the brown-coloured cake first appeared in Dijon in the Middle Ages. It became increasingly commonplace in the 18th century and Dijon then pushed ahead of Rheims as a producer of this particular speciality. The product is still manufactured today (750 tonnes per year), and its production is still small-scale. Adorned with delightful blue or pink decorations, it can be sold in the shape of a clog, a Christmas log, a bell, a fish or a snail.

Dijon wine

Dijon has left Beaune to become the wine capital of Burgundy but it has a few vineyards such as the former ducal estate at Marcs d'Or whose grape stock was moved to a site above Lac Kir by the Town Council in 1981. There is also part of the Montre-Cul wine-growing area between Dijon and Chenôve.

Wine Festivals

Every year at the end of August or beginning of September, the *Festival of the Vine* attracts young people from all over the world to Dijon and the Côte area. This tradition goes back more than fifty years. Some thirty folk dancing and singing groups from five continents take part in the *Folkloriades internationales de Dijon* in a dazzling array of costumes. The main centre is the Cellier de Clairvaux and an audience of 100,000 attends the festivities that end the week-long festival, on the Sunday. Prizes awarded during the competition are highly sought-after by folk dancing choreographers worldwide.

Front cover:
A general view of Dijon - The porch on St. Michael's Church
A house front in Rue de la Chouette - Square Darcy.
Glazed roof tiles.
Back cover:
St. Bénigne's Church.

Cartography: AFDEC, Paris

© 1998 Édilarge SA - Éditions Ouest-France, Rennes
ISBN 2 7373 2357 6 - Dépôt légal : mars 1998 - N° d'éditeur : 3745.01.2,5.03.98
Cet ouvrage a été imprimé par Pollina SA à Luçon (85) - n°74150B